Shahaama

Contemporary Issues in the Middle East

Mehran Kamrava and Carol Fadda-Conrey, *Series Advisers*

Praise for *Khul-Khaal: Five Egyptian Women Tell Their Stories* . . .

"These rich, personal histories, with the addition of a perceptive and detailed foreword by anthropologist Andrea Rugh, make *Khul- Khaal* an important contribution to the growing number of publications which seek to promote an understanding of Arab women's roles."
—*Africa Today*

"These life histories present some of the most extensive, direct, and intimate non-fictional portraits of Middle Eastern women available in English."
—*Middle East Journal*

"Their moving and often poignant stories shatter many of the popular assumptions that Western and Third World feminists alike have about the lives of working-class women."
—*Washington Report on Middle East Affairs*

"These are powerfully honest accounts of women's struggles from early childhood through adulthood told by those who have certainly thought about the course of their lives and the daily problems they are forced to confront. These sketches tell us that women are at the center of the family and that the family is central to social relations in society; therefore, women are important and count."
—*Journal of Developing Areas*

Shahaama

Five Egyptian Men Tell Their Stories

Nayra Átiya

Foreword by **Andrea Rugh**
Afterword by **Roger Allen**

Syracuse University Press

First Edition 2016

16 17 18 19 20   5 4 3 2 1

∞ The paper used in this publication meets the minimum requirements
of the American National Standard for Information Sciences—Permanence
of Paper for Printed Library Materials, ANSI Z39.48-1992.

For a listing of books published and distributed by Syracuse University Press,
visit www.SyracuseUniversityPress.syr.edu.

ISBN: 978-0-8156-3434-8 (cloth)
978-0-8156-1061-8 (paperback)
978-0-8156-5356-1 (e-book)

Library of Congress Cataloging-in-Publication Data
Names: Atiya, Nayra, author.
Title: Shahaama : five Egyptian men tell their stories / Nayra Atiya ;
foreword by Andrea Rugh ; afterword by Roger Allen.
Other titles: Contemporary issues in the Middle East.
Description: First edition. | Syracuse : Syracuse University Press, 2016. |
Series: Contemporary issues in the Middle East
Identifiers: LCCN 2015041343| ISBN 9780815634348 (cloth : alk. paper) |
ISBN 9780815610618 (pbk. : alk. paper) | ISBN 9780815653561 (e-book)
Subjects: LCSH: Men—Egypt—Biography. | Egypt—Social conditions—21st century.
Classification: LCC HQ1090.5.E3 .A85 2016 | DDC 305.310956—dc23
LC record available at http://lccn.loc.gov/2015041343

Manufactured in the United States of America

For
Samir and Nabila Atiya

and

In remembrance of
Asma el Bakri (1947–2015) and Shabramant

Egypt is not a country we live in
but a country that lives within us

—HIS HOLINESS SHENOUDA III,
117th Pope of the Coptic Church of Egypt

Contents

Foreword

Fans of Nayra's book *Khul-Khaal: Five Egyptian Women Tell Their Stories* (1982) have been waiting three decades for more oral histories. Now finally *Shahaama: Five Egyptian Men Tell Their Stories* is here with men's stories to complement those of the women. *Khul-Khaal*, with its lyrical women's stories, won a UNICEF prize in 1990 and has since been translated into seven languages. I expect the men's stories will enjoy the same popularity.

These stories reflect a time when norms and values in Egyptian society were more clearly defined and a person's reputation was a significant part of his or her sense of worth. If the men's stories were told in 2015 as they looked back to the 1970s, the decade of their young adulthood, it is doubtful they would retain the freshness and authenticity of that earlier time and place. The storytellers would almost certainly alter their narratives to conform to contemporary views of "old-fashioned" mores. Presentations of self invariably cry out for approval, and the approval these stories seek is lodged in a different time. Yet the stories remain relevant to present-day Egypt as its people go through the throes of a political transition. They show the discontents, obstacles, and hardships men faced in preparing themselves for their adult lives and the heavy responsibilities they had to assume in supporting their families. Whereas *Khul-Khaal* was relevant to a heightened interest in women's roles, *Shahaama* deepens our understanding of men's frustrations that led up to the 2011 uprising.

The stories are not told by scholars who guess at the unconscious meanings behind Egyptians' words or develop abstract principles about the way Egyptians think. These are real people presenting genuine stories that are narrated in the manner they choose to portray themselves. Although we can't discount the fact that the men present selective images of themselves, we can be sure these images coincide with what was believed to be noble at the time. Still, the men appear to be telling both the good and the bad in their lives and therefore the stories can be trusted as not straying too far from fact. Any small deviations come from individuals shaping their accounts in hindsight to give a more coherent storyline and purpose to their lives. Yet, that said, there are themes that reflect Egyptians' lives in a broader sense both at the time they occurred and now. Noting the themes may help readers know what to look for.

Urban environments play a compelling part in several narratives, even though some of the men spent their childhoods in rural environments. This was a time after Independence in 1952 when modern education was becoming a way for children of aspiring rural parents to move into the middle classes and away from the hard labor of agriculture. Once educated, graduates were guaranteed government jobs for life with secure benefits and salaries. These jobs were necessarily located in towns and cities and meant in most cases that the government could arbitrarily transfer employees from place to place and even abroad. For these men this life differed considerably from growing up and living a lifetime in a rural community.

Education created a new sensibility in people, not all of it good. Nayra found, as did I working in village projects, that one could count on the less-educated villagers to carry on more coherent philosophical and lyrically eloquent conversations. The illiterate cultivated a richness of expression and deeper understanding of life that was expressed in aphorisms, proverbs, and sayings confirming the irrefutable nature of the truths they described. No matter that other expressions equally validated the other side of the argument. The educated, by contrast, always seemed to be straining to find the "right" answers to questions posed to them. Even though most of the narrators were educated, their years out in the world seemed to have offset the disquieting lack of inquisitiveness that public schooling tended to breed in Egyptian children.

The women's and men's lives are recounted differently in the two books—at least partly because most of the women came from lower-class rural environments and the men from middle-class backgrounds. Both, however, grounded their stories in concrete examples—they "showed" as they "told" their stories. In *Khul-Khaal* the women's interests were embedded mainly in family concerns. Their lives as they saw them began with arranged marriages that they accepted with ambivalence—as a chance to fulfill themselves as women yet with anxiety about leaving their parents' homes where life was ordered and secure. Their childhoods, if mentioned at all, were a time of preparing for marriage—cultivating a modest, unassuming demeanor, a reputation for hard work, and learning the skills that make good wives and mothers. After they married their problems became those of failed marriages, poverty, and concerns about children. For them the world was a stark place of good and evil, where recourse to superstitions helped them survive.

The men's stories, by contrast, describe the hardships, hurtles, and corruption in the public world that had to be circumvented to get ahead. They related events in shades of gray, where sometimes it became necessary—even a victory—to manipulate the system in unseemly ways. Their stories teemed with the trials of schooling and later early adulthood when they had to amass the necessary enormous resources to marry and maintain the accoutrements of a middle-class lifestyle.

Men worked hard toward marriage, but from the little they said, one feels they too were ambivalent about this new stage in their lives. Those who could not meet the financial prerequisites of marriage broke with the women they purported to love, but once they met those conditions, they often married hastily without really knowing the women well. A man might even then be refused by the woman's parents if they felt he did not earn enough or his family background was not worthy of their daughter. If the man eventually divorced, he blamed the problem on the general greediness of women. The two Egyptians who seemed most satisfied in their marriages were the man who immigrated to America and married late and the fisherman who married his own choice—in both cases "irrational" love marriages.

Once marriage was achieved, all but the fisherman barely mentioned their wives again except to complain about them. Their focus returned to the burdens, now increased, of supporting families and overcoming the same hurdles that obstructed their way before. What made them reluctant to talk about their wives? Was it reticence to talk about their private lives? Were they simply staying on message that a man's life mission was to be a good breadwinner, model father, and upstanding citizen? Whatever the reason, they continued to deal with difficult superiors, faced arbitrary assignments, earned insufficient salaries, and experienced family crises that entailed ever-new responsibilities.

Indeed, although the men may have reworked their lives as best they could to make them success stories, in truth the bureaucracy was stacked against civil servants, making it difficult to define what success might be. This raises the question of whether men were not the ones having a harder time fulfilling their defined gender roles than women who elicited so much sympathy from Western audiences. The men were expected to support immediate family members, parents, and in some case elderly aunts, brothers, and sisters. The women, on the other hand, performed tasks that although arduous were nevertheless carried out with little interference and rewarded with approval when accomplished well. Perhaps most rewarding, women spent their time at the core of the very family life that meant so much to both men and women.

Despite the reticence of men to talk about their wives, it was clear that women played a key part in these men's lives. We know this from the glowing way they described their mothers, who were probably not so very different from their wives. From their descriptions we feel the women provided the quality attributes to family living, whereas the men were away battling the challenges of earning an income. Women offered good food and comfort and invariably were present to provide solace for the disappointments their children encountered in the outside world. Mothers were the teachers of wisdom, the unfailing supporters of their children, the keepers of confidences, and even the arbiters in children's differences with their fathers. They were the eternal refuge. From the men's tender descriptions, one concludes that every mother of the time was a paragon of virtue. By contrast, the men's relations with their fathers were complicated—fathers could be idolized models of correct behavior or demanding, unreliable, and disappointing, exhibiting behaviors that their children sometimes found unfathomable.

Both men's and women's presentations of themselves were meant to reflect on their own worth as well as on the reputation of their family. In a world of unreliable institutions it was the family's public standing that won business contracts, marriage partners, and needed favors. Men's conduct in addition reflected on their local communities, their religious denominations, and even on Egypt itself when they came in contact with foreigners. Those who know Egypt will recognize the values of loyalty, dignity, and respect that recur in Egyptian narratives. Although the men tell their stories as uniquely their own, they share a compelling interest in staying loyal to their social groups. Even the Jewish narrator speaks of Egypt with affection.

The men's stories do not speculate on the future, which from their perspective was in God's hands, but neither did they hesitate to prepare for it. They simply didn't plan future career paths too definitively for fear of tempting fate, but readily grasped the opportunities that unexpectedly came their way. It was only after extraordinary effort and dashed hopes that the men resigned themselves to what fate presumably had in store for them. Belief in destiny didn't cause passivity but rather gave them the ability to accept what occurred and move on. Perhaps this was a therapeutic way to meet devastating disappointments—a father's death, sudden poverty that halted a son's education, or the financial inability to marry a loved one.

What do these stories say about differences in religious backgrounds? Surprisingly little, it would seem! The men celebrated different holidays and related to coreligionists somewhat differently. One senses a Muslim majority that didn't dwell much on differences with minority communities, a somewhat inward-looking Christian community in terms of socializing, and a Jewish community that met frequently to observe rituals. In the Coptic story, Nader went to public school and thought nothing of having to study Islam and learn verses of the Qur'an. Religion played a more significant role for the Christian narrator only when he began looking for a marriage partner or for the Jewish man when he became an avowed spy for Israel. The latter went to jail and eventually was deported, but there seemed little animosity toward him on the part of his Muslim guards.

Clearly rituals and life events like marriage separated the religious groups, but they did not affect friendships or cause major divisions in school or in work—at least not to the extent that they do today. In the way the men present themselves, in their values, and in their general adherence to the mores of *shahaama* (gallantry), they were all similar. There is a genuine Egyptianness apparent in each one of them.

Egyptians are storytellers, as these oral histories show. The men predictably elaborate the good and are reticent about embarrassing details that might flaw the image. Nayra as an Egyptian has inherited the storytelling gene. We see this quality in the way she coaxes out details from the men, gaining their trust and overcoming their reluctance. She obscures their names to prevent embarrassment and elaborates details where it might make more sense to non-Egyptian audiences. The narrators provide the details while Nayra sets them in context.

The stories follow a format different from Western storytelling. The Western story builds to a final climax with perhaps a few miniclimaxes along the way. Egyptian stories proceed with a long chain of repetitive highs and lows that rarely reach a final dramatic resolution. For them this imitates life more closely—people don't marry and live happily ever after, rather they marry and have children, and these children have children, and life goes on. Art echoes this format in the geometric patterns on mosque walls with no beginnings or ends, or Um Kulthum's songs that go on for hours with no hint of when they will end.

Young Egyptians today in the throes of their revolution may not recognize all the details of lives lived in the 1970s but they will recognize the desires of these men to live secure, satisfying, economically viable lives grounded in the principles of justice, dignity, and respect, exactly the goals of the revolution. And readers will find in these stories reflections of the gallantry—*shahaama*—that is so characteristically a part of everyday life even now that it still instills a loyalty toward Egypt in the hearts of its people.

Woods Hole, Massachusetts   Andrea Rugh

Preface

In 1955, my family and I moved to the United States from Egypt. I was eleven. We subsequently visited Egypt only in summer, on vacation. In 1976, however, an opportunity took me back for an extended stay. By then, I was a young wife and mother. My family was offered as our first dwelling the *Fostat*, a huge retired Nile steamer. We fell in love with the boat and with living on the river. The *Fostat* was moored on the Giza side of the University Bridge in Cairo and was a dream home. When it was no longer available to us, my son Adam and daughter Katrina and I moved to downtown Cairo to the apartment building where I was born, constructed in 1929 by my maternal grandfather. This once-elegant five-story structure, four flats on each of its spacious floors, had fallen into disrepair. As rents prescribed by the government for rent-controlled apartments throughout Egypt were ridiculously low, owners could barely cover the cost of repairs or renovations and only the most necessary were effected. Despite its shabbiness and minimally functioning elevator, a coat of paint to the apartment helped, and we enjoyed our downtown home with its wrought-iron balconies overlooking the Egyptian Museum of Antiquities on one side and a Catholic school and convent on the other. From our front windows we watched the pink stone of the Antikhana neighborhood glow with the pollution-heightened colors of sunset. From our back windows, we saw the Italian nuns on their rooftop, strolling or hanging laundry, clad in long habits and snug wimples. Their convent's bell accompanied our comings and goings and in some odd way I was reassured by its deep tolling.

Our building was close to Tahrir Square, which had once been called Midan Ismailiyya and renamed Midan el Tahrir after the 1919 revolution leading to Egypt's independence from Great Britain in 1922. The name came into full-fledged use in 1952 when, in a bloodless coup, King Farouk was deposed and Egypt was declared a republic. After the events of 2011 and 2013 when President Mubarak resigned and President Morsi was ousted, it was dubbed "Martyr Square." Tahrir Square, when we lived there in the 1980s, though noisy and traffic congested, was certainly not a gathering place for revolutionaries. Rather, it was a hub for city buses and the site of the mugama', a twenty-story building that houses Egypt's sprawling bureaucracy. In 1943, when I was born, the neighborhood was clean and quiet save for the clatter of a passing streetcar, donkey cart, horse-drawn carriage (still in use), or an occasional automobile. "If it's a crimson one, it's the king's," a grownup explained, saying that this color was reserved for royalty and no citizen was allowed to drive a red car.

Nader Bestawros, the second storyteller in this book, recounts taking a last bus from Tahrir one day after a late evening with friends at a student and intellectuals' hangout, the Café Riche. He runs into a long-lost schoolmate fleeing arrest and shelters him for one night. The young man is a member of a Muslim Brotherhood family whose arrest (along with others considered insurgents) was ordered by President Gamal Abdel Nasser. Nader's readiness to help brought to mind the concept of *shahaama*. When I later asked for his interpretation of this code of honor, he responded: "It means you are generous, loyal, and have a desire and a readiness to help others. You do not let others down and you endeavor to safeguard their reputation. You keep your word, you do not speak out of turn and you act with dignity and courage."

I met Nader Bestawros in New York. He had by then become an American citizen. He was tall, had a full head of wavy gray hair, and a formal demeanor. He had strong opinions and was brusque at times, but loyal and generous to his family and friends. When I asked him if he had thought about the risk to his family when he sheltered his classmate, he said: "I could not do otherwise; we had eaten bread and salt together (*Kalna aysh we malh*)." He was referring to a cultural conviction, the enduring bond forged between those who have shared food, bread, and salt. It is only one of many convictions he held that made him so quintessentially Egyptian. Yet he eagerly left Egypt, explaining to me: "I carry Egypt and the Coptic church of Egypt in my heart, but unfortunately Egypt does not appreciate its own until they have left." Years before, my father had said the same.

I was the firstborn of my parents' two children. When my mother began her long labor she was assisted at home by Doctor Helena Sedaros, my maternal grandmother, Teta Katrina, and my great aunt, her sister, Teta Doussa. My father was in Alexandria teaching at the university he participated in founding in 1938. He was, at the time, also involved in the university's transitioning from a branch of Cairo University, then still named Fuad University after Egypt's King Fuad, to an independent institution, Farouk University. When, in 1952, it was renamed Alexandria University, my father had already resigned, having grown disheartened with the bickering and backstabbing he encountered among his colleagues, making it difficult for anyone to move to higher ground. Both Nader Ali and Nader Bestawros describe in detail the chicanery of jealous coworkers and colleagues, certainly the antithesis of *shahaama*.

Though my father was away from home as my mother labored on that March day in 1943, my maternal grandfather, Habib Bey

Messiha, was in residence but out of the house. My grandmother explained that he had fled his favorite child's ordeal. I am guessing he was chased out, as this was no setting for a man. I have black-and-white photographs showing my grandfather gazing adoringly down at his first grandchild, who laughs toothlessly up from a fold made of two massive armchairs pushed together. I still remember their chintz slipcovers, though I have no conscious memory of my grandfather who died in a tramway accident when I was nine months old. He was just eccentric enough to prefer public transportation to his chauffeur-driven car, and apparently missed a step while exiting the tram and was caught under its wheels. Teta Katrina told me that, at what must have been the moment of the accident, her wedding ring flew from her finger as she washed her hands in the bathroom sink: "I had an awful premonition before I got the news." She went into mourning and henceforth dressed in black until her death in April of 1969, shortly before my daughter Katrina's birth.

In 1976, it was exciting to return to Egypt as an adult; I looked forward to exploring it with my children, who were then seven and nine years old. When the Egyptair flight we had boarded in New York the night before began its descent into Cairo International Airport, there it was, "the city victorious," in all of its glorious dust and band of vivid green along the Nile, pushing away the desert.

The nearly twelve years spent in Egypt (1976 to 1987) changed the course of my life in many ways. For one, I quit an academic career for which I had trained in favor of the siren song of oral history and writing. I found a nation of storytellers whose delivery was pure poetry to my ears. I was eager to record anyone willing to speak with me, thinking all the while: if only I had been doing this before the elders of my family had died! I listened with the enthusiasm of one returning to a place once loved, drinking it in and getting to know it in a new way.

The memories I came to Egypt with in 1976 were mostly those of a child; family gatherings, excursions to the beach, historic markets, museums, archeological digs, sights of one sort or another visited mostly with family or family friends. We were rarely exposed to people different from ourselves unless they were in our service: priests, teachers, owners of businesses, among others. Such a one was Hagg Nounou, a spice merchant in the Mousky. I loved his name because in baby talk it means "tiny," yet he was tall, pale, lean, radiant in his impeccable kaftan and overcoat. As a girl, my mother, who was born in 1917, accompanied her mother to his hole-in-the-wall shop and took me there too when I was a child and Nounou old but vigorous. Like her, I remembered receiving a rock-candy treat suspended in clusters from a thin string after he had filled our orders. He wrapped them in brown paper bundles snuggly secured with thin red-and-white string. Nounou sold spices directly from his shelves and also mixed them fresh to order for clients, sending the ingredients to a grinder down the street, who pounded them to fragrant perfection in his giant stone mortar and pestle to match. Teta Katrina went to the Mousky twice a year for her spices, as did my mother before we left for the United States. My grandmother's signature recipe for *buhar* (allspice) is one I still have. When I get a whiff, I remember how we sneezed and sneezed breathing in spice and pepper dust as we sat waiting on the narrow ledge fronting Nounou's shop while he measured, mixed, called for the grinder, and chatted amiably.

It was thrilling to live on the Nile from 1976 to 1979. I enjoyed the open decks of the *Fostat*, the glassed-in salon on the foredeck and the spacious staterooms with bathrooms shared by each two rooms. The galley and the dining room were below, the windows decorated with macramé hangings I ordered from an American weaver then living in Cairo. Aft, on the upper deck, was a large open-air living room hung with sailcloth curtains, drawn in spring and summer against the afternoon sun. The sunrises and sunsets, the smoky air at dusk, and the moonlit nights on the water were unforgettable. City lights winked at the river after dark and twinkled all night in its velvety water, making us feel we were living in a giant jewel box.

I spent days observing life on the river and taking note of life on the street above us. Beyond the gangplank, leading from the lower deck of the *Fostat*, was a small lawn bordered with daisies, marigolds, and nasturtium, shaded by a tall rubber tree. Over time this tree spread its branches and glossy leaves above the lantana, which flanked the steep stone steps leading to the street and a retaining wall made of the same stone. There, courting couples sat chatting and pedestrians stopped to rest, gaze at the river, or stare. They were no doubt as curious about us as we were about them. Cairo's heartbeat was fresh to my ears those first years on the *Fostat* and I drew inspiration from its fount of life.

Speaking first with women, I tape recorded, transcribed, organized, and wrote their stories into what became *Khul Khaal: Five Egyptian Women Tell Their Stories*. Being inexperienced at the time, it never occurred to me what valuable documents these audiotapes were. And, yes, today I blush to say that I recorded over recorded interviews and discarded tapes after the stories were published. When next I interviewed men, I got only as far as transcribing the tape recordings. Life (for lack of a better word) got in the way of my writing them up, and over several geographical moves I lost the tapes; luckily, I recovered the transcripts. I chose five stories. Although I don't think that *Shahaama* can be considered a companion book to *Khul Khaal*, I used the same book-building approach: interview by listening more than questioning; transcribe tapes word for word, making comments on mood, tone of voice, pauses, hesitation, excitement, sadness; organize the transcripts by color coding themes and by cutting and pasting; enhance text with explanations, proverbs, sayings, songs, historical detail, and personal experience where relevant; write the stories up; revise, revise, revise; toss out all but the finished product, a task I avoided later. In 2006 when I finished writing *France Davis: An American Story Told*, and this life of the Reverend France A. Davis, pastor of Calvary Baptist Church in Salt Lake City, Utah, was published a year later, I offered him the tapes we made together.

I began tape recording women's stories when my interest was piqued by snippets of conversation or chatter I heard on the street, from neighbors, people who came to work for me, or with whom I interacted in one way or another. I relished their use of colloquial Arabic, which I understood and spoke. I loved the energy, imagery, and detail of their storytelling. Likewise, I was engaged by the men's stories and collected these in Egypt, Europe, and the United States. I chose these five: Nader Bestawros, an Egyptian Copt and academic who emigrated to the United States; Mohammad Maghrabi, a Muslim fisherman who never left Egypt; Youssef Salman, a Jewish businessman who grew up in Alexandria and emigrated to France; Nader Ali, a Muslim attorney with rural roots who never left Egypt; and Ali Kamal, a Muslim city boy, production manager, and filmmaker who traveled outside of Egypt for work and always returned.

The first man I recorded was Mohammad Maghrabi, the fisherman whose wife Naima's story appears in *Khul Khaal*. The couple moored close to us and eventually invited me to step onto their rowboat for a glass of tea. I reciprocated by sending them food from our galley and minding their boat when they traveled to their village in the Delta, often at feast times. Mohammad detailed and demonstrated methods of fishing on the Nile and I wrote a feature article for *The Egyptian Gazette* with the information gleaned from him. "Fishing on the Nile" was published March 20, 1979. When later he added his life story, I combined the two. As a fisherman his story naturally revolves around fishing, methods of fishing, and living on the water. Though he talked about his rural beginnings, his parents, his brothers, customs and superstitions, how he came to be on the river, how he met and married Naima, and their only daughter, Reda, his life's purpose was fishing and fishing was his story.

In the mid-1980s my children returned to the United States to continue their schooling. I stayed behind and soon decided to leave the noise and pollution of downtown Cairo. I bought a piece of land near the village of Shabramant, between the Giza and Dahshur pyramids, and got ready to build a house, a project that helped me to weather the loneliness I felt without Adam and Katie. It was because of this land purchase that I met Nader Ali, interviewed him, and subsequently wrote his story.

Nader Ali knew real-estate law. A friend recommended him, saying, "If you are buying agricultural land and dealing with peasants, he's your man. He really understands their mentality and will make sure everything goes smoothly." She was right. I took him to see the area and meet the sellers. This spot appealed to me because it was verdant and peaceful, near enough to the magic of the desert that I loved, less than an hour away from Cairo, and near friends in the neighboring village of Haraneyya. Nader was indispensable to me in the course of negotiations. As it turned out, parcels of land I wished to buy belonged to one set of siblings, whereas thirteen date-bearing palms growing on it belonged to another. Two brothers owned the dirt under the trees; three sisters owned the palms and collected precious income from their date harvests. The sisters were reluctant to sell; the brothers were of another mind. And I, in full-fledged innocence, went back and forth between them until Nader came to the rescue. Had he missed the palm-tree discrepancy I would have bought the land unaware that the trees were not included in the purchase price. I cringed to think how I would have been mired in a mess not unlike the one described in the cautionary folk tale "Musmaar Goha." One of a myriad of Goha stories, it tells of the wily rascal who sells his house but manages to retain sole ownership of one nail within its walls, which he can visit at will.

Once I had the land I hired an architect and contractor to help me design and build a house with domes, vaulted ceilings, polished brick floors, Arabesque windows, and doors made by a local carpenter. I drew inspiration from the traditional style revived by the Egyptian architect Hassan Fathi, using stone instead of time-honored mud bricks with blush-and-earth-toned stucco applied to the surface. The inside walls were white-washed. There was no electricity or water on the property, so I dug a well, installed a pump, put in a septic tank, and applied for permits to get power. Like experiences related by the men in this book, I soon found out the meaning of bureaucracy, learning also that courtesy and a little oil to the gears did much to keep things moving. There was only a narrow dirt path leading to the house. When power cables were delivered and left at the top of the main road, a friend, who was building a house across from mine, took matters into her intrepid hands. She hired men to dig trenches, attached the cables to the back of her Russian-built jeep, and pulled them in to power up both our homes. Mine was a two-bedroom, two-bathroom arrangement with kitchen, dining room-study, and an airy living room with built-in sofas, a wood-burning fireplace copied from a nineteenth-century house, and an antique church door refinished for a coffee table. A pair of enclosed courtyards opened to the sky and doors led to the fields, where I soon planted orange and lemon trees, artichokes, loose-leafed Egyptian cabbages, turnips, and other vegetables, rotating the crops with alfalfa and the *berseem* (clover) that carpets the Nile valley in brilliant green during one of four growing seasons. The flat roof was ideal for stargazing and the setting perfect for solitary evenings with a book or the company of friends. This is where Nader told me his story over the course of two years. In winter I recorded indoors and on warm nights we talked in the courtyard, palms waving in the breeze above the walls and the tape recorder running. Nader got the first dates harvested from the thirteen trees I had nearly forfeited.

Nader was a devout Muslim, traditional in his values but also liberal in many ways. He was not above enjoying an occasional Scotch and water while we recorded, even though Islam forbids the consumption of alcohol. I discovered quickly that he was a keen observer of people, a philosopher and a compelling storyteller. In his deep rasping voice he spoke about family, friendship, challenges, politics, men and women, his dreams, his ideas on marriage and raising children, accidents, life and death. Smoking his long Cleopatra cigarettes, he told me how he was certain a friend was dying when he noticed the shape and color of his nose had changed. Adding a proverb to make a point, as Egyptians often do, he said, softly, *"al dunya fanya wal zaman ghaddaar,"* loosely meaning: life is a passing dream and time waits for no one. *Kana'a*, equanimity or acceptance, was a concept he held dear: "Whether you have a rich feast of *dik rumi* (turkey) or a simple plate of *ful medammes* (fava beans), it's all the same and you are no longer hungry after you've eaten. It's not your stomach grumbling that it is not satisfied," he liked to say. He felt that acceptance leads to gratitude, which leads to peace of mind and happiness, even in difficult times.

I think Nader would have elaborated on his life story had I not been called back to the United States to attend to a family crisis in December of 1987. When he came to say goodbye, I entrusted him with deeds to my property and other legal documents. I was sure I would soon be back, but destiny had other plans. I was gone for over a decade. When I returned I looked for Nader and learned he had moved to an office near the Giza Pyramids. I called and visited him and found him to be much the same Nader: at once gracious and gruff, gaunt, elegant, high strung but now sporting a cane, as did I. We laughed about it, agreeing that it was a useful and fashionable appendage. In view of my silence, Nader could have disposed of my papers, but he took pride in his loyalty. When I said that I now made my home in the United States near my parents and children, he handed me my dossier and helped me to bring closure to my concerns in Egypt. This was an example of *shahaama*.

I met Youssef Salman through a Jewish friend who had also grown up in Alexandria and moved to Paris in the 1960s. Youssef was born and raised in Alexandria, attended Zionist youth meetings in the 1940s, and was arrested and eventually deported. His departure coincided with a huge Jewish exodus in the 1940s and 1950s. His parents were not among them: "We were born here and we will die here," they declared. As the Jewish community (eighty-thousand-strong at one time) dwindled, they became increasingly isolated and eventually died in a home for the aged, like a handful of others who would not be moved. Interestingly, Youssef did not tell his story much beyond Egypt, offering glimpses of what life was like for a middle-class mercantile family in Alexandria, among others who made Egypt home but never took out Egyptian citizenship: the Greeks, Armenians, Italians, Croatians, Spaniards, British, French, Maltese, and Russians, to name a few. I was asked why I would include his story, since, though born in Egypt, he identified himself as a European and a Zionist first and foremost. As I see it, he represents one of the many faces of Egypt, providing a noteworthy vignette of a moment in its history and the history of one of its once-vital communities.

I met Ali Kamal while working on a film. I was impressed by his gentle manner, diligence, honesty, loyalty, and quiet confidence. To me, he too embodied *shahaama* because of his courage and his readiness to help and stay true to his word. A devout

Muslim, he had liberal ideas and a lifestyle to match. He belonged to the generation of Egyptians that was deeply affected by *al naqsa* (the setback, calamity)—the defeat of Egypt at the hands of Israel in 1967. Younger than Nader Bestawros and Nader Ali, his story adds to theirs and provides a background for events taking place in Egypt today. Like theirs, his story encompasses a generation's concerns through the lens of personal history.

On impulse, Ali Kamal married a woman who seemed a good match. When she decided to wear the *hijab* (the veil) two years after their wedding, he tried to dissuade her but failed. He said, "Wearing the *hijab* changed my wife and caused a rift between us, but we stayed together because of the children. Some wear the *hijab* out of conviction and because it lends an air of respectability. Many do so also because it saves money on clothes and the hairdresser. Mind you, it's a fashion too, as demonstrated by the burgeoning shops and boutiques specializing in *zayy islami* (Islamic dress)."

Ali Kamal served in the Egyptian Army. He empathized with all soldiers and told me that he was moved to tears by the song of a young Israeli who had lost both his legs on the Syrian front. He had time to think while on duty as a wireless operator in the bowels of an army tank in the desert: "The youth of my generation believed in a republic of Egypt and in Gamal Abdel Nasser's leadership. We listened to songs such as *Batal al Thawra* (Revolutionary hero) and sang Gamal's praises, calling him the father of our nation. We were certain he would lead us to victory, but instead we were blindsided and suffered a defeat that altered our lives forever." Ali was referring to Israel's attack on and destruction of the Egyptian Air Force in 1967 while its planes were still on the ground.

Because their dreams were crushed, sadness and depression afflicted Ali and many of his peers. However, he always brightened when speaking of the patriot, singer, and icon Um

Kulthum: "She gave voice to our feelings and was the voice of Egypt." Like Nader Ali, Ali Kamal described how not only Egyptians but also people throughout the Middle East waited for Um Kulthum to sing on the first Thursday of every month, many flying in for her concerts. Both described how they memorized her songs, which were published ahead of time in the newspapers. They described how families gathered around the radio listening raptly to her repeat a phrase and later watched her on television, equally enthralled. Ali Kamal's description of Um Kulthum would have met with the approval of every Egyptian, I think. He said: "She was a picture of dignity, of Egyptian womanhood, her signature handkerchief clasped in one hand, her black hair gathered in a bun, her long dress perfectly tailored, a diamond crescent brooch pinned to it. She was 'the lady,' our lady. She was unique." The singer and film star Abd al Halim Hafiz was a favorite too, affectionately nicknamed al 'Andaleeb al Asmar, the dark song bird or dark-skinned nightingale, because of his beautiful tawny complexion and his beguiling voice. He too sang patriotic songs but above all he spoke to the romantic hearts of Egyptians and gave voice to their emotions.

Nader Ali's, Nader Bestawros's, and Ali Kamal's stories have threads in common that are visible in the detailed descriptions of their lives, thoughts, and physical surroundings. Their values too are similar, as they are steadfast in the certitude that their word is their bond. Youssef Salman in his way displayed *shahaama* by not betraying the camp guard who helped him during the time of his internment. The guard repaid the favor by finding a way to covertly return confiscated personal property to him as he stood on the deck of the ship that took him away from Egypt forever. This was the guard's act of *shahaama*.

Mohammad Maghrabi fiercely protected his little family, kept a vigilant eye on his fellow fisher folk, and also on my children and me when we were alone on the boat. Although his story does not give concrete examples of the concept, I know he acted with *shahaama*.

I have replaced real names and places to protect the identity of the speakers where necessary and when requested. I chose names for the five men in this book to suggest the cultural subtleties communicated by names and to reflect the three main communities of the Egypt of the storytellers. I chose names close to the storytellers' own to help me remember the real storyteller and not slip into fictionalizing him. Like the two Naders here, the real Naders had the same first name, a name shared by Christians and Muslims alike. Their family names alone indicated their religion. As to Youssef Salman, his real name was not clearly a Jewish name, leading me to pick an equally nebulous name to identify him in this book. Ali Kamal adopted his father's first name as his last, and for this reason I mirrored him. Mohammad Maghrabi wanted his real name to be kept.

Names are first indicators of where to place someone and are particularly significant identifiers in a culture where religion is key, a sort of passport. Unless your name labels you clearly, people will ask as a matter of course and without reticence: What is your religion? Because my name could be Muslim, Christian, or Jewish, I was always asked. Additionally, first and last names are often interchangeable, like Nader Ali and Ali Kamal. This is because people typically identify themselves (or are identified) using their father's first name as their own last name, or their father's and grandfather's first names as their own last names. My father's first name was Aziz and his father was Suryal. Thus, I am referred to in Egypt as Nayra Aziz or Nayra Aziz Suryal, only sometimes as Nayra Atiya. Imagine the confusing possibilities when identity papers or legal documents are issued or needed!

The men spent much time talking to me about their childhoods, family life, school years, and friendships as they were growing up. These were the happiest years of their lives, the most vividly remembered and eagerly revisited. Thus I gave weight to childhood years when writing their stories. Of course, to varying degrees and in different ways, they talked of becoming men, their hopes and dreams, their sensitivities and quirks, education, employment, love, marriage, the search for their place in society, political awareness and economic struggles, instances of religious or economic discrimination they encountered, obstacles placed in their way because of their class or religion, their personal philosophies and ways of coping with life.

Whereas Mohammad Maghrabi's life as a fisherman on the Nile seems timeless, I believe that Nader Bestawros's, Nader Ali's, Ali Kamal's, and Youssef Salman's stories offer us insights and help us to better understand twentieth-century Egypt. Can their personal histories shed some light on the twenty-first century? On how current events unfolded—the 2011 and 2013 uprisings, for example?

In organizing and writing the stories I deleted repetition where necessary and transliterated Arabic words and phrases casually, as I heard them rather than using conventional or scholarly guidelines. I believe that oral history allows for this flexibility. I rearranged and fleshed out events and personalities and added detail to enhance or clarify the narrative. I did not deny my own voice and experiences when I felt that ornamenting the story would enrich and not alter it. Above all, I made every effort to stay true to the storyteller's voice and to the spirit of his story.

I hope that you will find these personal histories as genuine and engaging as I have. May they offer you a vivid picture of times gone by and a better understanding of an Egypt alive with change.

Acknowledgments

My gratitude and thanks to the encouragers who did not waver over the years, to the ones who stepped in along the way, and to those who live on in memory.

Shahaama

Nader Ali

My hometown of Qutur al Mahatta is located between Kafr al Shaykh and Tanta on the agricultural road linking Cairo and Alexandria. Tanta would have been the "big city" for us children growing up in Qutur and was at one time the regional administrative center for thirty-three villages. Qutur al Mahatta (Trains' Station) is a railroad town and the name of the town reflects this.

Prince Mohammad Ali, Prince Consort before King Farouk of Egypt's son was born, owned large tracts of land in the area. The nazir, or overseer, of his estate lived in the town of Biltag, about 3 kilometers from our home. Once a month, his wife invited the wives of Qutur's civil servants, town officials, and businessmen to visit her and to spend the day in her grand home. The nazir's wife sent a horse-drawn carriage to fetch the ladies early in the morning, and they spent the day socializing over breakfast, lunch, and tea. At sunset they returned home by carriage. My mother looked forward to these visits, which offered a welcome break from her daily housekeeping routine and responsibilities. These women all knew and visited one another, as they were of the same social class, the middle class. Their husbands were civil servants: the chief of police, the telephone station-master, the postal and health services employees. Others were married to doctors, merchants, or business owners and tended to be richer and live in the biggest houses.

1

My father was a government employee and the first telephone stationmaster in the village of Qutur. He was born and grew up in Tanta and was sent to Qutur when telephone service to the village was installed, which, interestingly enough, was before electricity was available in the village. No ordinary citizens had private phones and everyone went to the telephone office to make or receive calls. My father placed local calls directly from the Qutur office but routed long-distance calls through Tanta. Anytime you went by the open door of the telephone office you heard people shouting into the receivers, as if it was the only way to be heard across a great distance.

The railroad administration built many of the houses in the village of Qutur. I remember in particular a cluster of ten designated for white-collar workers and another eleven, built on the outskirts of the village, for laborers and their families. The houses for laborers had one bedroom, a bathroom, living room, and kitchen. Their foreman's house, however, had two bedrooms. Other government-built houses were designated as services buildings, such as the telephone office, post office (the postmaster lived above), health clinic and dispensary, and the police station. Some houses were reserved for the use of visiting doctors who came periodically to treat a population plagued with schistosomiasis, also called bilharzia. It is one of Egypt's greatest health problems, spread by parasitic worms and infected fresh-water snails. Farmers and fishermen whose hands and feet are constantly in irrigation ditches and contaminated waters are most at risk, many succumbing to repeated infection that destroys the bladder and intestines and kidneys, eventually leading to death.

In the 1920s the Egyptian government mounted a campaign to educate and treat such infected populations, and in the 1930s and 1940s the Ministry of Health set up tent hospitals throughout the countryside, including one in Qutur. These hospitals stayed three or four months in a given location, then were moved to a new town or village. However, medical services ramped up when there were epidemics, like the cholera epidemic of 1948, and the tents stayed in place longer. I remember the epidemic. It was terrifying to see neighbors taken away and mattresses, bed linens, and personal effects thrown out of houses and burned. People wailed day and night as ambulances carried away men, women, and children. Luckily, my family was spared.

The year of the cholera epidemic, the Ministry of Health sent a worker to the village to teach people the basics of hygiene and how to prevent infection. We followed his instructions to the letter, placing a basin of water with Detol, a strong disinfectant, outside our house and washing thoroughly before entering. My father went straight from work to our shed before setting foot in the house. He undressed, washed, disinfected, and changed into clean clothes and then came in. Mother sprayed his suits with Flit, a bug spray made with DDT that she also sprayed in the house and shed using a hand-held pump (I remember it as yellow in color) that she refilled periodically. She boiled clothes and did all laundry with lye soap. She boiled water for drinking and washing vegetables and fruit, adding permanganate of soda to kill any germs, especially on leafy greens vegetables and romaine lettuce, the only kind we had.

Schools closed for a time that year and children were kept indoors until it was declared safe to go back. I remember that my grandmother, Sitti Um Saber, my father's mother, walked from Abu Lula, the next village over, to check on us in Qutur when she heard the news of the epidemic. She clutched me to her breast and refused to let go when I squirmed and tried to wriggle free. It was as if she believed that her arms could ward off the disease. I was her favorite grandchild.

Mine was an ideal childhood. Despite my family's modest means, our life was sweet and peaceful and we enjoyed a sense of well-being. We enjoyed fresh air. Egypt's land was rich and fertile and four crops a year insured that even the poorest could pick greens out of the field, grab a couple of tomatoes, a handful of onions, a crust of bread, a little *gibna bayda* (feta cheese), a bowl or sandwich of *ful medammes* (fava beans), and not go hungry.

We had rituals associated with daily life, religious feasts, and the seasons, and we children had a lot of freedom to run around, to explore and play outside of school. Our roles were clearly defined and understood, both in the family and in the community, and our lives simple and well ordered. There was a predictable rhythm to our days and a balance that made us secure and happy. I have not since experienced such peace.

Our house was small, clean, and comfortable. We had plenty to eat and were clothed and cared for. Our parents told us to hold fast to our faith and taught us how to pray five times a day. They reminded us to trust in God and encouraged us in our pursuits. They expected us to do better than they did and to go on to secondary school, even to college. Also, friends egged each other on and helped each other. I had a wonderful group of friends, the likes of which I've never since been able to replicate. We cared for one another.

My father was a civil servant and my mother a housewife. They had eight children and chose names for seven of us starting with the letter "N": Nader, Nassar, Noha, Nagwa, No'man, Nahed, Ne'mat, and Nadia. When my mother told people that she was expecting an eighth child, they advised her to give the baby a name starting with a different letter. Three children had died in infancy and it was whispered that it was because of spells cast on them by ill-wishers, the evil eye of the envious, or maybe even because of the repeated use of the letter "N." When my youngest sister and the last of my parents' children was born, my mother named her Hala.

Three months after Hala's birth my parents sent my sister Nagwa and my brother No'man to live with mother's two unmarried sisters. Our aunts lived in Tanta, an hour away from Qutur by train. I do not know how this agreement was reached, but my aunts assumed full responsibility for my siblings. They informally adopted Nagwa and No'man and enrolled them in school in Tanta. My aunts no doubt satisfied their maternal instincts, but the arrangement served perhaps to relieve my parents of a burden, raising so many children on my father's modest salary.

Even though our family's resources were limited, I don't remember ever feeling like anything was lacking. Mother was a good manager and supplemented my father's income by growing a vegetable garden, raising chickens, rabbits, and ducks, feeding them with all the scraps from the kitchen and letting them otherwise run free in the yard to pick the ground for seeds and grubs. The chickens laid eggs, of course, which it was often my job to gather from under the bushes and shrubs. We also had four fruit-bearing tees: guava, orange, lime, and mango. The mango bore *manga hindi* (Indian mango), which is yellow in color, slender, and thin skinned with a small pit surrounded by juicy sweet flesh. Sometimes after eating a mango I planted the pit. They sprouted and two grew into trees but none bore fruit. My father bought beef or lamb from the butcher only on feast days; otherwise we ate what we grew or raised. The garden was mother's domain and, when she could, she sent a hamper of food to the children and my aunts with anyone from the village traveling by train to Tanta. Nagwa and No'man enjoyed the bounty, but the longer they lived in Tanta the more they grew to despise the country and our country ways. They called us "backward." They had electricity, whereas we had gas or oil lamps. They said soot went up their noses and blackened their fingers, whereas I took pride in polishing the glass globes and enjoyed the soft light. I was used to the bugs, but they complained about them whenever they visited. Over time, they restricted their visits to feast days.

I still own our house in Qutur, even though I now spend much of the week in Cairo because of work. Whenever I can get away, however, I do because there is no place I love more, no place I feel happier and where I feel so at peace as in Qutur al Mahatta and the house in which I grew up. It was really the happiest time in my life.

As I approach the village, I imagine the voices of my childhood friends and playmates. As I push open the garden gate, I remember chasing after eggs from our chickens in the hedges and under the bushes. When I put the old-fashioned brass key in the front door, which leads directly into the old *sala*, our family room, my family is there in spirit. The divans are the same ones we sat or napped on, their flowered chintz slipcovers are the ones my mother made, though they are now worn and faded from many washings. I am reluctant to replace them. The table where we sat to eat is the same table and the beds are the same. When I throw open the shutters, the creaking of the wood is familiar and so is the perfumed night. The smell of wood smoke and flowers enters the room and instantly I relax. This is home, where I spent my happiest years.

The house is a very simple one. It is built of limestone and brick, with thick walls and good insulation. There are two long windows in the square family room and the window wells show the depth of the walls. The front door is a double door with half-glass windows and iron grills that can be opened for ventilation. The *salon*, that is, the parlor, not the family room, was kept closed unless we had visitors. On one side of the family room is my parents' bedroom, which is now mine, and on the other side is the second bedroom where the children slept. There is a small kitchen and a small bathroom that had an unusual triangular first landing inset with a Turkish-style toilet and an area for bathing on the other side. We used a washtub and pitcher when I was growing up. I have since renovated the bathroom, installed a regular toilet, a shower, and a butane water heater.

Like all Egyptian families living in the country, we made our own bread. My father's unmarried sister lived with us and helped with baking on the first Thursday of every month and also with other household chores. Outside the house was a shed and a room for baking with a domed mudbrick oven. On special occasions, my mother made *aburi*, a regional delicacy, a small round bun with a cavity in the middle. Buns were taken out of the oven when half baked, a lump of clarified butter and a raw egg broken into the cavity, and the bun replaced to finish baking. *Aburi* for breakfast was one of the most delicious foods I have ever eaten. Some people in the region put butter and sugar in the cavity instead of an egg.

To celebrate feasts it was customary to bake *kahk*, a sweet cake stuffed with a mixture of dates and honey called *agamiyya*. The house was upside down for days before the feast as cleaning, laundry, cooking, and baking took place. Kneading the dough, preparing the *agamiyya*, pounding the sugar with which to dust cookies and cakes when they came out of the oven took time. The sugar came in solid cakes; pounding it was my job. Mother sometimes gave us small lumps of dough to make dolls and allowed us to decorate them with the brass serrated tweezers used to pinch designs in the *kahk* before they went into the oven. On the day of the feast they were served with coffee, a special treat. Sending *kahk* to others to wish them a happy feast was the custom in families who could afford to do so. Family and neighbors exchanged plates of *kahk*.

Bread-baking days were among my favorite days when I was growing up. I loved the baking preparations and the process. Auntie Mazuza always came to help. She was not family, but a widowed neighbor whom we addressed as "auntie" as a show respect and even affection. She was poor and proud and refused money for her efforts, but accepted rice, sugar, tea, clothes, anything my mother had to spare. Mother always said something to let her know that her help was a favor we appreciated. I know she enjoyed her visits and being needed and we enjoyed having a useful elder in the house. Older people and younger people interacting gave life special flavor.

Auntie Mazuza arrived early on Wednesday and stayed until Friday. She, my mother, and my aunt Sakina, my father's unmarried sister who lived with us, got up at 2 o'clock in the morning on Thursday to knead the dough and prepare the oven. They made lumps of dough and left them to rise, then they flattened each one for a second rising, making flat, round loaves of our traditional *baladi* bread, like pita but darker and chewier. From time to time, they made a paper-thin flat bread with corn and wheat flours, adding a small amount of *helba* (fenugreek) to the dough to strengthen the blood, they said. *Helba* produces a body odor I dislike, though I enjoy this crisp bread we call *bettaawi*. My mother made a batch without *helba* for me. Later, I found out that *helba* is also used in some Indian curries.

On baking day the aunties fired up the oven with twigs, bits of wood, dung patties, whatever was on hand. The dung patties are the most common fuel in the villages. Dung is collected from livestock, mixed with straw, and dried on the rooftops. It burns well and has a sweet smell. On this day there was flour everywhere, loaves going in the oven and coming out, bread spread out to cool on every surface. No one cooked that day, but *ful medammes* was prepared the night before and slow cooked all night in the *fawaalah*, a potbellied urn. We ate it any way we liked: dressed with oil, lemon juice, salt, and pepper, or with shatta (cayenne pepper) and cumin, or with clarified butter (*samna*), salt, and pepper. This was our meal on baking days, with fresh bread, of course. It was a meal from heaven!

My mother kept a couple of days' worth of soft bread on hand and hardened the rest of the loaves in the oven after cutting them down the middle to look like half-moons. This hard or dry bread we call *aysh naashef*. It is meant to keep for a month or until the next baking day, and is stored stacked in hampers, covered with a clean old dress or sheet. To soften it, we dipped it in water or gravy.

Early Wednesday morning, family and neighbors set out together in search of a donkey cart for hire. Several families loaded the cart with burlap sacks of wheat, corn, and rice and we took these to the communal mill for grinding. We made a day of it, each family using the grinding machine in turn, stopping in the middle of the day to eat lunch together. After a grinding cycle was complete, women placed their hands over their mouths and ululated. These *zaghareet* of joy were the signal for the children to come forward and beat and drum on the sides of the machine to release the chaff and bran that stuck to its walls. Some of the chaff was used to feed the animals and the bran was added to the bread, sprinkled on the bottom of loaves ready to go into the oven. Not only is it very healthy and full of vitamins but it also keeps the bread from sticking to the floor of the oven. "Never waste anything," my mother said. We did not.

At the close of day at the mill, we were white from head to toe. I felt such excitement and exhilaration as we refilled the sacks with flour and loaded them back on the donkey cart and started for home! Once the sacks for each household were unloaded and the donkey cart returned, mother and the aunties organized for the next day. Much as I loved these baking days, I hated the cleaning up afterward and escaped the house if I could get away.

I heated water, took a bath, drank a glass of tea, and donned my freshly washed and pressed pajamas to go out strolling with my friends. Young men such as myself—sons of functionaries, civil servants, members of the middle class—went out dressed in this way as long as we were walking around the village or in the fields.

My friend Maurice's mother was the village seamstress and came to our house to sew pajamas for the boys and nightgowns for the girls. We thought of the pajamas as leisure suits, and although we never went to school, to work, or away from the village dressed like this, they were our rural uniform for relaxing. When I was a little boy they were cotton pajamas and when I grew up they were made of silk woven in the Upper Egyptian town of Akhmim. My mother or auntie Sakina washed them and I ironed them making sure I made a pencil-sharp crease down the middle of the pant leg. I felt fresh and natty as I stepped out to stroll with my friends. Only the boys went out at night, however. The girls joined us in the daytime to play or study. For our night strolls, we gathered at one or another of our houses and set out together to stroll through the village or out into the countryside on full-moon nights. In summer, we never went home before midnight.

Such rituals and such times leave a profound impression that stiffens the backbone, helps you weather life's difficulties. The sweetness of them even in memory is like strong tea with lots of sugar that feeds the muscles of weary peasants after a hard day's work in the fields. They give us a clear sense of self and confidence in our strength to endure. Of course, faith in God gives us the ultimate strength.

A distant relative of my father lived in the village of Abu Lula, where my paternal grandmother also lived. One of my fondest memories is of Sayyed Ragab sitting under a huge white mulberry tree, telling stories. He worked all the while, making ropes or hampers with fronds and fibers trimmed from his date palms. He also made tools and baskets in which the dates from his harvest could be transported in August and September. Every part of the date palm was used.

"When I was a boy," he always began, "I played in the trees. Climbing was second nature to me, and I learned to climb, prune, pollinate, and harvest. Everything I learned, I learned from my father. In the month of *amsheer* (March and April) the *khamseen* (strong desert winds) swept the countryside like a stiff broom. He said of this month, *amsheer abul hawa wal za'abeer Amsheer,* father of winds and storms. It was time to prune back the trees and use the stubs to climb and fetch the pollen-laden pods from the male trees and climb the females to insert the pollen in their budding clusters. Of *baramhaat,* April, he said, *baramhat, ruh al ghayt we hat,* go to the fields and gather. This was because vegetables were ready to harvest."

In July and August, we watched him go up the trees with a *mitla',* a wide belt used for climbing made from the reddish-brown fibers of palm trees. He slung it low across his hips and around the tree, tying it securely. Then, leaning back into it, holding both sides of the rope, he pitched up the stalk, one stump at a time, feet splayed on either side of the trunk, the date palm swaying all the while. He carried with him a round, flat harvesting basket secured on three sides by a triangle of short ropes, linked to a very long rope that allowed him to lower it to the ground once it was heaped with dates. On the ground, the women stacked the fruit in *gereed,* rectangular baskets like small cages made from split palm limbs lined with palm fronds to keep the fruit from falling out and to protect the dates. We had learned how he made the *mitla'* by observing. He rubbed the palm fibers between the palms of his hands until they formed a twist of rope, adding fibers and rubbing the strands between his fingers to make an ever-increasing length, which he attached to his big toe to keep it taunt as he continued the process. You could say that he was growing a rope.

I felt a little queasy sometimes as I watched him inching up the tall trees on a windy day carrying the clusters of pollen to the female trees. When I asked him how the male pods did not just blow away, he said, "I upend them into the female pods and tie the pods shut with slivered palm leaves to keep the strands from falling out. Did you know that one male pod can pollinate four females, Nader? A successful harvest depends on this and if pollination fails the dates are nothing but hard pellets, good only for animal feed. Did you see the clusters I gathered up in my lap? The females took every last one of them and this year's dates will be like drops of honey!"

School was a very important part of our everyday life. We went to a beautiful school called The Railroad School, a few minutes' walk from our house. It was constructed along with the railroads to serve the children of government employees and of course railroad workers. I will describe it for you. Our classrooms were made of cement slabs and the walls were supported by concrete columns. I can tell you that although it looked nice, the school was cold in winter and hot in summer. Concrete does not insulate well. We attended school from September to June, leaving home at seven in the morning. Before we left, mother served us hot, well-sugared tea with milk, and when 10 o'clock came around we had a break for breakfast and at 1 o'clock another one for lunch. Everyone went home for breaks and meals. There was no school uniform as such, but there was a dress code. Boys wore shorts, white shirts, white socks, and black shoes. Girls wore dresses, smocks, and black shoes.

As a child, I was very sensitive about my appearance and I still am. My mother often told stories about how I refused to set foot outside the house unless my clothes were freshly laundered and pressed and my shoes shined to a high gloss. The headmaster of the school was my role model. He looked like the singer and movie star Abd al Halim Hafez, whom we lovingly called the dark nightingale, *al 'andaleeb al asmar*.

The Railroad School was coeducational. We were twenty-five boys and girls in class and we all went through the grades together. My school years are my happiest years. Our group at school was diverse, both socially and economically. Some, like the doctor's children, or the children of a rich businessman in town, lived in fancy houses. Some, like my family and other families of civil servants, lived in comfortable but modest houses. Our classmates whose fathers were laborers had even more modest houses. We got along and our interactions were free and natural and we looked out for one another too. Of course we were aware of our differences and of our social ranking. I can tell you that my friends Ahmad and his sister Aziza were at the top of the ladder because their father was the doctor. Nana was next because her father was a well-to-do businessman. I was third in ranking because my father was a civil servant and wore a suit to work. As to Maurice and his sisters, they came next. Like my father, their father was a civil servant but he had died, leaving the burden of their care to their mother. This dropped them a few rungs on the social ladder because their mother, once widowed, sewed for a living. She sent both of her children to college, however, and they cared for her as she aged.

Maurice was my closest friend and I often went to visit him at his house. Others of our group came too. We watched his mother work late into the night sewing by the light of two oil lamps, especially before feasts when everyone wanted new clothes. The lowest man on the social ladder was our friend Sayyed. He was the son of a railroad worker, a laborer. Despite the fact that he stuttered, he was the best student of the lot. We all liked him and cared a lot about how he was treated. You know, I have to chuckle at times when city folk call us backward. I feel we were better integrated than city dwellers. Boys and girls of our group were together at school and at play. We were respectful of one another, we roamed until 10 or 11 on summer nights and our parents did not fear for our safety. It came as a shock to me when I found out that boys and girls in Tanta did not mix freely, that they were inhibited and wary around one another. In fact they rarely mixed until they got to college, and even then they did so awkwardly.

I had an accident and broke my chin in my second year of primary school. It was a freak accident. Here's what happened. A cousin of my mother's was a farmer who owned livestock. He lived about 5 kilometers from Qutur. His water buffaloes were healthy and he often brought us rich, whole milk. There was nothing called pasteurized milk or milk in cartons or bottles at that time. It came directly from the animal and it was raw milk. My mother boiled it and we drank it. Or she let it sit until *ishta*, cream, rose to the top, then skimmed off a layer that had formed as thick as a pancake and put it on a plate for us to eat with honey and bread. Sometimes we ate it with *meshaltet*, a pastry like bread with multiple layers, dripping with *samna*, clarified butter mother made at home. She also made cheese, rolling it in bamboo mats to form logs. Just about everything we ate was homemade or homegrown.

But to get back to the accident. Mother's cousin rode a donkey from his village of Abu Lula to Qutur to visit us. He always tied his donkey to a post outside the house, and one time I untied the donkey and took a ride along the railroad tracks, on the steep embankment. Suddenly the donkey took fright when a freight train blew its whistle, bolted, and threw me off, right in the path of an approaching train. I landed between the tracks just as my friend Sayyed's father was walking home. He froze and shouted to me to lay still. "Don't budge, don't move, stay where you are, stay flat," he shouted just as the train approached. I did and the train passed over without hurting me. In the course of the fall, however, I broke my chin. The donkey did not wait to see the

outcome and must have hightailed it back to Abu Lula. Abu
Sayyed took me home and told my parents what had happened.
I was chastised for having taken the donkey without permission
and my uncle walked back to his village that night. Until he died,
he reminded me of this incident.

All in all, we grew up in a time of peace and stability, a time
where values were clear, outside influences few, and trust and
concern were expected. We knew our neighbors and people kept
an eye on each other's children. We knew what was expected of
us, and the courtesies of daily life were well defined and familiar to us all. These ordinary lives we led as children were really
a precious gift and a privilege. Dire poverty notwithstanding,
they provided a secure base on which to build self-reliance and
resilience. They were, you might say, leavening for the future. We
knew who we were.

One of my happy memories is of the games we devised and
played as children. An irrigation canal ran near our house. We
played in the fields around it and our playground was really about
three acres. We played hide and seek and, on uncultivated bits,
kura shurab, a game using a ball made by wrapping old socks
and stockings around a tennis ball until it reached the desired
size. One year we decided we wanted to try tennis so we created
a net with bits of string we collected and saved over time. We
made imitation rackets with wood, and when volleyball caught
our interest next, we simply raised our tennis net on sticks and
adjusted our game. We made up games too and fabricated our
own toys. Nothing was store bought, and I believe that creat-
ing our own entertainments kept our minds active. We liked to
make cars using found wood or cardboard and Coca Cola bottle
caps collected from around the cold drinks merchant's bright-
red icebox. It had a silver bottle opener bolted to the side. Every
bottle cap dropping to the ground from every bottle he sold
and opened went to making car wheels. We punched holes in

them, strung them on wire loops and attached them to our little vehicles. The steering wheels we made also by looping wire and wrapping it with discarded fabric scraps. We pushed and pulled our cars, raced them, and imagined all the while that we were really driving. We made whistles from reeds or paper, sometimes even from bits of lead used to seal loaded freight cars that had been discarded or dropped around the depot. We begged the stationmaster to let us have them and he did. We made kites with discarded newspapers and reeds cut from the banks of the canals and irrigation ditches, and we made paste with flour and water and attached fancy tails from string and shredded paper. We took pride in our creations.

Summer was our favorite time of the year. We were out of school and our gang of kids roamed the countryside at will. We packed an alcohol burner, a couple of glasses, the tiny blue and white enameled tea pot my mother reserved for outings, tea, sugar, and some food. Old burlap sacks sewn together for us by Maurice's mother and attached to sticks served as a lean-to for shade. Sometimes we hunted birds, made a fire, and roasted and ate them bones and all. We brought bread and cheese from home and scavenged the fields for arugula, *gargeer* (scallions), *basal akhdar*, *khiyaar* (cucumbers), and *oota* (tomatoes). We gave the farmer tea and sugar in exchange.

My friends and I had one favorite excursion destination. It was called the *ma'atah*, a field divided in small squares planted with a variety of vegetables. The farmer who owned or rented such a field usually set up a small shelter for himself and spent the summer there, tending his crops and making sure they were safe from plunder or mischief. We children liked to visit with him and he let us pick a few ears of corn to roast on his fire. We made tea and shared it with him; also we shared anything else we happened to have. It was a worry-free time, a wondrously happy time. Oh, the freedom we had!

Before 1964 and the completion of the Aswan Dam, the Nile flooded yearly in the months of *abib* and *misra* (August). The thirsty fields drank the water and steam rose up, making the air hot and sultry. We loved this time despite the humid heat. The river was high and vigorous, the canals brimming with water. It is hard to explain the feeling that I had, the feeling that we all had, I think, when the water rose and the very air seemed fertile with hope. It is the closest thing to euphoria that I have ever experienced. My friends and I cut bamboo, made rods and traps, and went fishing. If we caught small fry, we cooked it on the spot. If the fish was of a good size, we took it home to our mothers. Sayyed was the best of us with the rod and traps. He took home the most fish, and we understood that God provided for one with the greatest need. God is great, *allahu wa akbar.*

One summer a tagalong followed us to the river and wouldn't take a hint no matter how we tried to shake him. We probably wouldn't have minded except that he was jealous of Sayyed's fishing skills. After once too many times tangling our friend's lines or wrecking his traps, we grabbed this fellow by an arm and a leg and heaved him into the canal. He came out dripping and lunged at Sayyed, but we pulled them apart and he finally left us alone.

Sometimes mothers sent us out in search of *mulukhiyya*, which grew like a weed on field edges or among cotton plants. It is prolific. In summer, starting in *bashant* (June), peasants were glad to be rid of it. Egyptians love the mucilaginous bright-green soup made from its leaves, considering it a national dish along with *ful medammes* and *kushari*. It is made with chicken or rabbit broth and typically eaten with rice, hard or soft bread, and raw, chopped onions dressed in vinegar. The meat is extracted before chopped *mulukhiyya* leaves are added to the broth. My mother lightly browned the chicken or rabbit in clarified butter, sprinkled the pieces with salt, pepper, and allspice (*buhar*). She then arranged them on a serving platter to be eaten separately. I love the aroma of the pepper and the cinnamon and cloves in the *buhar*, and when I get a whiff I am transported back to my boyhood days.

In preparation for making *mulukhiyya*, aunt Sakina washed and removed the stems and chopped the leaves. Mother would already have killed and cleaned the chicken or rabbit for the pot, adding a whole onion to the water as well as a couple of nuggets of gum arabic (*mistikah*) to perfume the broth. Auntie then spread the leaves out to dry on a clean bed sheet on a bed or divan, as you must never chop the leaves when they are wet. When ready, she prepared the chopping block and the half-crescent-shaped blade with two handles called the *makhrata*, going back and forth over the leaves until they were chopped to her satisfaction. She then tossed them into the soup along with minced garlic fried in *samna* and gave the soup a quick boil before serving. I just remembered that years later, after I had moved to Cairo, an Italian told me that they called the *makhrata* a *mezzaluna*, meaning half moon, and that it was used in Italy as well. Because *mulukhiyya* is a soporific, we napped directly after lunch. How delicious it was to feel replete, to go into the quiet and cool of the shuttered bedroom and sleep!

Another of our activities as children was bicycling. We rented bikes from 'Am Gad, paying him a couple of piasters an hour. Riding like the wind made us feel powerful. Of our friends, Aziza was not allowed to go with us, as her father thought it unbecoming for a girl, especially a doctor's daughter. Aziza and her brother Ahmad were more strictly controlled than the rest of us. If they could not join us for some activity, we just descended en masse on their house. Their father could say nothing to this. It would have been rude to chase us out.

During summer vacation, my friend Maurice and I rode 18 kilometers more than once from Qutur to Kafr al Shaykh, leaving in the cool of the afternoon and returning at sunset. We rode on a dirt road at first, and when the road between Kafr al Shaykh and Tanta was asphalted, we were excited because we could ride faster and farther. A paved road meant opportunity, meant we could go places, even ride the bus. Our world expanded and the horizons before us were limitless.

I hated seeing my year in fourth grade come to an end, as this meant the end of primary school and the end of childhood. It also coincided with a period of financial distress for my father and a painful setback for me as a result. My father told me that he would not be sending me to secondary school in Tanta as planned. I was miserable. All of my friends were going and I would be the only one left behind. I had to settle for the Ilzami-yya School, a five-year teacher-training institute in Qutur, and I wanted nothing to do with teaching or being a teacher. But there was nothing to do about it.

Once I started at the Ilzamiyya, I systematically cut classes. I went to school for morning roll call and slipped away as the students filed in. When the headmaster took notice, he told the janitor, the *farraash*, to grab me and take me to the town barber to shave my head as punishment for what he called my vagrancy. I kicked and tried to break his stranglehold on me, but to no avail. I felt humiliated and ran home and went straight to bed. I refused to answer my mother when she asked me what happened, nor would I accept food or drink from my aunt, who tried to soothe me in this way. My siblings also worried, knowing that I was high strung and of a nervous disposition. I refused to respond and began to burn up with fever. I closed my eyes and waited for my father to come home. I wanted him to own up to his mistake in sending me to the Ilzamiyya, but he did not utter a word. I waited for him to say anything, but he was silent. Later, I understood that he was sad because he had no choice but to have me stay where I was and finish the year. Finally, when he spoke, he said to me: "Nader, my son, you will not go back to that school and until we can think of what to do you can come to work with me." And so as soon as I recovered, I went with him daily.

As it happened, a friend of my father who worked in the ministry of education dropped by to see him at the telephone office one day. My father greeted him, saying, "*Itfaddal ya Uthtaz*, Abd al Hakim, please have a seat and a cup of coffee." Mr. Abd al Hakim was surprised to see me out of school and could tell that something was troubling my father. He asked, "Why is Nader here, Saber Affandi?" And my father told him. Mr. Abd al Hakim said: "Listen, Saber Affandi, your son Nader is a good boy. He should study at home and then sit for the secondary school exams in Tanta at the end of the summer. Send the boy to me as soon as you can and I will talk to him about this. I will see what I can do." And so I went.

Mr. Abd al Hakim greeted me kindly and questioned me about my likes and dislikes. I answered, and he was very gentle and explained my father's predicament, saying that he had recommended I study at home until it was time to sit for exams and then take them. He would see what he could do to get me a place at the school in Tanta. Hearing this, I felt as if a black cloud had lifted. I thanked him and went home and told my father what had happened.

When he saw my father again, Mr. Abd al Hakim said, "Saber Affandi, I will send you as many of the necessary textbooks for Nader as I can. You plan to buy what I can't send and let's get the boy started on the home-study course so he can take the exams. I'm sure he will do fine and then he can join his friends at school in Tanta." I remember his words as if they were spoken just yesterday, so great was my relief at his intervention on my behalf. He had been understanding and had rescued me, turned my life around, and relieved my father of the burden of guilt I now realize my father felt.

As planned, I began the home-study course. Nana and Maurice, Ahmad and Aziza, and the gang came to my house daily, or I went to theirs to study. They explained their lessons to me, shared their notes and helped me every step of the way. June came and with it the intense heat of summer. Even though they were on vacation, my friends did not go out to play much, but spent hours with me, helping me to prepare for my forthcoming exams in Arabic, English, math, history, geography, religion, art, health, and hygiene. And, in August, as the Nile began to rise, I sat for the exams.

My father insisted on coming to Tanta with me for the first exam. He waited outside the classroom. I didn't want him there, but couldn't tell him not to come. As soon as I came out he began to question me: "How did you do? What were the questions? Did you have any trouble?" Finally, I exploded: "Leave me alone!" I am sorry for this now, of course, since I have become a parent and understand my father's concern. The memory of this experience, however, taught me what not to do with my own children. My daughters know that they can speak to me whenever they wish and when they are ready to talk about exams or anything else, but that I will never question them. I don't always succeed, but I make every effort to let them come to me.

The week after the last exam, the results of the exams were posted on a bulletin board inside the school. I went to Tanta and was dumbfounded to see there were two Naders on the list with the same identifying number: Nader Ali, a Muslim, and Nader Girgis, a Christian. One of us had passed and the other had failed. What to do? The examining board wanted us to sit for the exams a second time, but Mr. Abd Al Hakim, who was in charge, said no. "They cannot be put through the rigors a second time because of your negligence," he told them, and instructed them to pass us both. This is how one Nader pulled the other Nader through and how we both attended school in Tanta that fall. Interestingly, we never became friends. In Tanta the boys and the girls were separated, unlike in Qutur, but we enjoyed the train ride and got together in the village. Some of us rode the trains on reduced fares because our parents were civil servants or worked for the railroads, and therefore special dispensation was made for us. This helped to ease the financial burden that my going to Tanta imposed on my father.

My mother had somehow put aside some money over a period of time, and before I went to Tanta she built a pigeon cote. She still had her chickens and they laid about thirty eggs a day. Aunt Mazuza collected them now instead of me and sold them at market, she and my mother sharing the proceeds. At that time, I was getting 10 piasters a week allowance from my father and I appealed to my mother to let me do chores to help out. She agreed. I cleaned the pigeon cote, collected the guano, and sold it as fertilizer to peasants growing watermelons and cantaloupes. By the end of the year, I had earned about 10 Egyptian pounds. I then asked her to let me do the ironing for the family. The *makwagi* who did the work in his ironing shop charged my mother 2 piasters to iron a shirt. I said she could give me 1 piaster, and she agreed. She had taught me to iron and I was good at it. I devised a table for the purpose, covering it as needed with a quilt and an old sheet, and set aside a day for the job. I heated the flatirons on the Primus after cleaning the heads with a special tool. If soot accumulated on the heads the flame was unsteady and inefficient. When the heads were maintained the Primus started up with a whooshing sound and a bright-blue flame. I ironed shirts, dresses, nightgowns, pajamas, taking special care with my own silk pajamas. At the end of the month, I presented mother with a list of what I had done and she paid me.

I also worked with my father at the telephone office a few evenings a week after school. The evening shift was 4 hours long. My father was proud to show me off to his friends and sometimes even left me to do the job alone after I mastered the switchboard. Typically, we went to the office at 6 o'clock and at 8 he walked the few steps to the village coffee shop, *al ahwa*, to join his friends, leaving me to do the job. The coffee shop was one of the few places in Qutur with its own telephone, and I could reach him if I needed him, and he could check on me. On such nights we had our routine, and I expected his call promptly at 10 o'clock to end the shift. He would say, "Nader, extinguish the oil lamps now, lock the door, and go home."

My friends knew my schedule at the telephone office and often came to sit with me, to talk or study, and of course to drink tea that was brought over by the cafe's gofer, a boy with a goofy smile and a slightly withered hand whom we nicknamed Billya because he seemed to move like a game marble. This love of togetherness, this antipathy to being alone, this certainty that we needed one another to survive was typically Egyptian. We have a name for it: *wanas*. It is one of our defining traits and an integral part of our culture, as is our sense of humor. Togetherness is expected and enjoyed. Of course, there are exceptions and eccentrics, but most Egyptians thrive on togetherness. We are by and large a gregarious, openhearted, friendly people, we Egyptians!

My father's first name was Saber. He was careful and courteous in his interactions with others, and all who knew him respected him. They addressed him with the Turkish title of Effendi or Sir, used for men of the learned professions. People pronounced it Affandi, in the Egyptian way.

Because my father made a point to say a thoughtful word or two to the operators in Tanta before making any request to put through a call, they expedited long-distance calls for him, and clients appreciated this. The respect and appreciation clients and operators had for my father naturally extended to his son, me. The operators came to recognize my voice on the nights I sat in for my father. They chatted and joked with me, teased me and called me *al affandi al sagheer*, the junior sir. One day, however, an operator who did not know me came on the line, and as I began to banter with her, she said brusquely: "Stop wasting time on the telephone and get back to work!" I made a cheeky reply and she insulted me: "What did you say, you son of a bitch?!" Of course I related the incident to my father, and he told me we would go to Tanta to smooth it out the very next day, which was a Friday. My father knew her schedule and knew she would be on duty that afternoon. So we took the train to Tanta after noon prayers and lunch and walked under the huge dome of the Tanta railway station, where the telephone office was located. The office was called *centrale al telephonaat*, or just *centrale*, from the French, meaning central telephone office.

We arrived in Tanta, had a glass of tea, and went to see this operator. My father, using the term of respect *abla* before her name, asked her, "Do you know who this is, Abla Laila?" She answered, "I've not had the pleasure, Saber Affandi." My father paused for effect, then said, "This is the son of a bitch!" She flushed, but my father put her at ease and an unpleasant situation was averted. After this, she was always pleasant to me on the telephone.

When the fourth grade ended we lost Ahmad and Aziza. Their father was transferred to Kom Hamada, then to Cairo. We also lost four others in our group, the children of the secretary of the Ministry of Health, who was transferred to Upper Egypt. The railroads assigned a new stationmaster to Qutur, however, who brought with him his wife and two sons, William and Fuad, and three daughters, Nana, Linda, and Mariam. They fit in from the start. We went to see them and extended a welcome and were soon playing together. We built a swing to hang from *shagaret al toot*, a huge mulberry tree in their yard, which we had designated as our clubhouse, and we climbed it, eating juicy white mulberries. We had a wonderful time. All kinds of things changed after that summer, however, and our lives changed too. The Education Act of 1953 provided free and compulsory education for children ages six to fifteen, and the nine years of basic education was split into six years of primary education and three years of secondary education. When I first started school it was four years of primary education. Our class was the first graduating class affected by the new act. I had lost one year at the Ilzamiyya and therefore had only two years of high school. My family prevailed on me to move to Tanta and live with my siblings and aunts while I completed high school. I could easily come home on holidays and for the summer. I was not keen to do so but really had no choice in the matter. I hated not commuting with my friends from Qutur and felt robbed of their companionship. And they missed me. I did not see eye to eye with my aunts or my siblings to start with, and increasingly found the confines of the apartment stifling. I escaped by going with my books to the Sayyed Badawi mosque for dawn prayers and to sit on the open-air roof to study or think. It was a time of reflection and a place where I felt the presence of God.

Al Sayyid Ahmad al Badawi, may peace be upon him, was a Sufi saint who came to Egypt from Morocco, having received a spiritual command to migrate to Tanta in the holy month of Ramadan 634 AH. Many who visited him there benefitted from his presence and his teachings, and to this day a festival in honor of his birth, *Mulid al Sayyed Badawi*, draws thousands to Tanta every year.

At the mosque I befriended a boy whose grandfather was a *shaykh*, a Muslim cleric and spiritual leader in this community, and we became pals. We met for prayers, watched the sun rise over the city, studied until it was time to leave for school, and walked there together. We also made it a habit to recite lessons to each other in order to memorize them. My friend invited me to his house, which was close to the mosque, and I met his grandfather, who told us stories about Al Sayyid al Badawi: "Al Sayyid al Badawi likened the poor in spirit to the fruit of the olive tree, some great and some small. He was like oil in the lamp of the faithful and invoked God's blessings upon them, encouraging them in their time of need." Al Sayyid al Badawi's mosque became my refuge in Tanta.

In high school, I acquired some hobbies and expanded my activities. I started collecting stamps and the high school counselor put me in touch with an American boy who had the same interest. I wrote letters that the English teacher corrected, and he helped me to read Edward's responses. For three years we traded stamps, and then our correspondence grew less frequent and one day stopped. Schools had facilities then that they lack today. We read magazines sent to us by various foreign embassies, and it was in one of these magazines that my teacher had found Edward's request for an Egyptian pen pal and suggested I write to him.

I also started a program of questions and answers over the loudspeaker at school, inviting fellow pupils to submit questions to the school psychologist. Yes, there was even a school psychologist in my day! I collected the questions and answers, then read them aloud over the loudspeaker every Thursday morning before classes started. My voice had deepened and I was told that I projected well. I was approaching manhood.

My relationship with my family in Tanta became tenuous, but out of a sense of duty and because I contributed materially to the household by living with them, they did not want to relinquish their hold. My mother sent weekly staples and supplies from the country, which they would not get with any frequency had I not been there. Early on I had told them never to question me about my comings and goings and they had agreed, but we were not at ease with each other. An ugly incident occurred before the end of the first year in Tanta, with irksome consequences. I will tell you the story.

A woman we called Abla Fatma lived across the street from my aunts. Mustapha, her husband, was an ambulance driver. They had a son and six daughters. Each daughter looked as if she had been stamped out of a different mold. No resemblance existed between the sisters whatsoever. Whereas Zaynab and Amriyya were beautiful, the other four seemed to have been forgotten by God in this respect. One of the daughters was divorced and living at home with her baby daughter. The rest were unmarried. Their brother, Mahmud, the oldest of Abla Fatma's children, was a layabout, addicted to hashish. Mustapha smoked it too, but managed to hold down a job. Mahmud contributed nothing to the household and a significant part of the meager income they had went up in smoke. Despite the hardships she endured, Abla Fatma had a kind word and a smile for everyone and never failed to ask after my family and my studies. One day she mentioned that her youngest daughter, Zaynab, was doing poorly in school and asked if I would tutor her. In Qutur, I was used to us boys and girls being together and thought nothing of this request. I accepted and started helping Zaynab two afternoons a week. Suddenly, my aunt's vitriol was unleashed and she used Zaynab as an excuse to castigate me. I had noticed that she was growing more pinched, her displeasure showing. I said nothing. One day, however, I returned home from tutoring Zaynab and she began to hurl insults on me: "You'll never amount to anything with that Zaynab hanging on your coattails," my aunt shouted. I was stunned. Without a word I gathered up my things and flew out of the house. How did I get to the train station? How did I buy a ticket or board the train or get off the train? I have no idea. I was in a daze. Somehow I got to Qutur and collapsed at the door of the house. When I came back to my senses, I was in bed, the anxious faces of my parents, my aunt Sakina, and some of my siblings peering down at me. They had called our friend the doctor, who examined me and told them that I had suffered a nervous breakdown brought on by some shock. I was to be kept quiet in a darkened room for twenty-one days. My parents complied.

Summer was approaching and so was exam time. My future depended on how well I did. My scores would determine if I could go to college and, if admitted, what faculty I would qualify for admittance to. In Egypt, a college faculty accepts you according to your exam scores. For example, those with the highest scores can go into medicine, whereas those with the lowest scores must accept archeology or commerce. It is a flawed system that does not consider the interests or capabilities of a student.

Once more, as I was recovering at home, my childhood friends rallied around me, as did one of the teachers from Tanta, a woman in her forties called Abla Samira. She visited me once a week on her own time to tutor me. She imparted wisdoms about life and gently coached me on ways to keep my composure in difficult situations. She also said that Zaynab was not responsible for what happened and that she and I should be friends, just like I was with the girls in Qutur. "Don't allow ugly tongues to dictate your actions, Nader," she said, and invited Zaynab and me to go to a tea garden with her when I felt better. I knew I could never really be friends with Zaynab but I obeyed Abla Samira's advice and agreed to go out with them once or twice. That is as far as it went, although Abla Samira was very kind and brought food to share with both of us when I returned to Tanta. I think that she understood our confusion as teenagers. Also, because she had no children of her own, she found satisfaction in taking us under her wing. Her kindness aroused in me feelings of respect and friendship, but it was also more than friendship. What I felt for her was love.

Finally the time for exams came. I sat for all of them and only got a score of 50 percent, just passing. Since the Education

Act of 1953 was passed, and with it opportunities for free education, there were a lot of youngsters like myself graduating from public schools, many with mediocre grades. Though I had passed, I had not done well enough to qualify for college and was sad. While I was considering my options and thinking of how to redirect my steps, events took an unexpected turn that again would change the course of my life. The Ministry of Education decreed just then that graduates who failed in no more than two subjects were eligible for admission to the national universities anyway. Consequently, some sixty-five thousand students applied and got in.

Here is what happened. The Ministry of Education insisted that Egypt needed more democratic, more realistic standards for university admission. In 1959, although ten thousand students had gained entrance to the national universities, some fifty-seven thousand had been turned down and had nowhere to go. Parliament voted to create a new category of student to accommodate those left behind: independents. We would be absorbed into the system but could only attend night school and could not sit for exams. This caused confusion and disparity but it was at least a foot in the door. I told my father about what was available to me and, knowing his resources were limited, offered to work and study. My father then decided to move me to Cairo and arranged for me to live with his brother, my uncle Fayid, and his family. As soon as I was settled, I looked for work and stumbled on an announcement in the newspaper that caught my attention. It was a recruitment call from the Ministry of Health, inviting high school graduates to apply for newly created positions as hospital superintendents. I went directly to the Ministry on Midan Lazughly, presented my credentials, and sat for the requisite civil-service exam and passed. Soon I was called to report for work at the Abbasiyya Fever Hospital and at the same time I was admitted to the Faculty of Law at Cairo's Ayn Shams

University. The Fever Hospital was close to Ayn Shams and so I took a leap of faith and accepted both. Since I was an independent student, I qualified only for night school, but I wanted more and wondered how to attend daytime lectures as well. So I did what every Egyptian does, I asked my friends Ahmad and Aziza for help. Ahmad was now a student at Cairo University and Aziza was married and lived in Cairo too. Their uncle was head of campus police at Ayn Shams.

I asked Ahmad and Aziza to speak to their uncle, and they were able to obtain a pass to allow me on campus during the day. The campus was not open to anyone and you had to show an identity card to get in. I was able then to walk to campus from the hospital and sneak into the daytime lectures while still performing my duties at the hospital. And I attended night school.

Abbasiyya Fever Hospital shared 70 or so acres of grounds with the historic Abbasiyya Mental Hospital established at the end of the nineteenth century. They were surrounded by beautiful gardens with old, well-established trees, and a tall, wrought-iron fence circled the entire property. I organized myself at work, performing most of my duties before going to lectures at the law school, praying all the time that my absences would not be noticed. After lectures, I returned promptly to complete my work at the hospital. This worked for a while until a mean-spirited coworker reported me.

Abbasiyya Fever Hospital had a big staff, including six superintendents, jobs that had been created after the 1952 revolution. In the years prior to the revolution, male nurses worked their way up the ranks to become superintendents, even though most had only primary school educations. The Ministry was determined to battle corruption in the ranks by attracting a better-educated citizenry, notably high school graduates. The goal was to build a conscientious staff base and to make these healthcare professions more respectable for those working in them who were not doctors. Nurses, orderlies, and nursing assistants were looked down on and carried out their duties grudgingly. It was a fact that the sons and daughters of "good families" would never become nurses or orderlies despite the Ministry's efforts to improve the image of these professions. Nurses, orderlies, and nursing assistants still do not get the pay or the respect they deserve, and because of the disregard they labor under they expect and accept gratuities from patients' families or bribes from coworkers, and seek out other ways to line their pockets. It is a sad situation to this day.

When I came on as a superintendent at Abbasiyya Fever Hospital, the older staff members resented me. Their ambitions and their years of service had been stymied by the Ministry's new hiring practices. These older workers found themselves suddenly supplanted by youngsters like myself, sometimes half their age, who became their bosses. A superintendent's take-home pay, although less than 10 Egyptian pounds a month, could net him as much as 150 Egyptian pounds if he took bribes, gratuities, and supplies. He might turn a blind eye to misconduct or trade in home-leave passes, promotions, better jobs, anything. He could skim off the top when dispensing supplies, food, or medications and sell them for personal gain. I refused to do this and consequently discovered not only that my youth worked against me in their eyes but so did my honesty. I came to be known as a straight shooter, which earned me the respect of the doctors but the distrust of my fellow workers and inferiors. Because they were helpless to change the course the Ministry had set and could not retaliate openly, they grew their arsenal of underhanded weaponry. They appeared to be courteous but conspired behind the scenes and stabbed you in the back. And that is just what happened when a male nurse saw an opportunity and reported my daytime absences to the hospital director, Dr. Rafik.

Dr. Rafik called me in one day just as I was getting ready to leave the hospital. He reprimanded me and relieved me of my duties at the hospital. Since, in Egypt, you cannot fire a government employee, he recommended I be transferred to a hospital in Upper Egypt, to Qena, 800 kilometers from Cairo. This was tantamount to banishment. Qena was a hardship post that no one wanted. I tried to persuade Dr. Rafik to reconsider, explaining and illustrating how I carried out my duties and fully compensated for the few hours I attended lectures at Ayn Shams, but he would not relent. Years later something similar happened to him because of the inflexibility of his character and, lo and behold, we both ended up in Qena.

Eventually, as the nation adjusted to becoming a republic, a problem arose between President Gamal Abdel Nasser and the minister of health. The president removed the minister from office and put an army officer in his place, General Mohammad Nassar. In my opinion, Egyptian hospitals never functioned better than they did under General Nassar, but he was disliked and feared. People worried about what they said in public, and the general had ears everywhere. He monitored what was going on from his office on Tahrir Square and also by making surprise visits, sometimes incognito. A word from him was an order. A hospital director could be transferred to Qena, for example, and this is just what happened to Dr. Rafik. When I got to know Dr. Rafik and we became friends, I understood that it had been his refusal to compromise, maybe even to flatter, that had caused him to fall from grace. He saw things as black and white, and we were in some respects alike for this reason. If you did not bend, you broke, and perhaps it has always been this way and always will be.

When Dr. Rafik arrived in Qena I thought he was on an inspection tour. Little did I know that he was there to be director of the Qena Fever Hospital. When he saw me, he looked surprised and said, "Are you still here, Nader?" "Welcome, Sir," I said. He asked, "Have you graduated?" I told him I was still studying. He just nodded. I offered him tea, but he refused, saying he was going to the hospital rest house to wash and change, and invited me to join him later in the afternoon. I was apprehensive about working under him again, but secretly pleased he had got what I considered his comeuppance. As it turned out, he became one of my chief encouragers, stopping after rounds to say, "Good morning, Nader. How are your studies? Do you need anything? Are you applying yourself? When are your exams?" and so on. Was this an expression of regret at what he had done to me, I wondered? Eventually, I understood that he was sincere.

My adverse experience at the Abbasiyya Fever Hospital was an important lesson I would not forget, and Dr. Rafik's inflexibility served as a lesson on what to avoid doing whenever possible. Before my transfer to Qena, I did something I regret to this day. Each ward at the Abbasiyya Fever Hospital had seventy to eighty beds. I coordinated visiting hours, a task that each of the six superintendents carried out in turn. It was our responsibility to insure that people came and went in orderly fashion. We also monitored families to prevent them from camping beside the sick patient's room, cooking, leaving food there, and jeopardizing the patient's recovery. This was especially critical in a fever hospital where individual cases of infectious disease could become an epidemic. It was a huge undertaking to get families to comply and to leave when visiting hours were over. They argued, they pleaded, they shouted, they wailed; some left, hid in the gardens, and sneaked back in. The hospital countered by retaining a dozen mounted police to herd them off the grounds before locking the gates. One day I was vacating a ward when a mother refused to leave her son's bedside. I was deaf to her pleas and blind to her tears; I had her forcibly removed from the hospital. In her mother's heart she must have known that her child was dying, and he did, just after she was carried out. I knew then that I had made an error in judgment. I had insisted on the rules without regard to humane considerations. I vowed never to harden my heart in this way again. When I got to Qena I made sure I did not forget this lesson and also promised myself that I would not forget school. I will tell you more about this later.

But first, let me go back to the Abbasiyya Fever Hospital and tell you a little more about this time. I was attending Ayn Shams when I fell in love with a fellow law student from Alexandria. Amira lived with her aunt and was everything I liked in a girl. She was calm, reserved, yet genuine. She was kind and generous, thoughtful and pretty. If you offered her a *ful medammes* sandwich costing a nickel, she made you feel as if you'd given her a turkey dinner. She was exactly my height, fair whereas I am dark, hair straight and brown whereas mine is black and kinky, eyes soft brown whereas mine are black and piercing. She looked like one of the Egyptian sculptor Mukhtar's feminine renditions of a countrywoman, perfectly proportioned, serene, and stately. We were opposites, but something drew us to each other and we fell in love. Amira acted as if she had been waiting for me all her life when we first met. She was without guile, a trait that appealed to me and was lacking in so many other girls. She made no pretense of it being an accident when we ran into each other. One day I saw her come out of class laughing with her girlfriends. They stopped to watch an organ grinder and his performing *maymoon* (baboon). They were just outside the campus gates. I followed them and teased, "Can't you ladies spare a penny for this man and his *maymoon*?" Amira turned and looked at me with a sort of mysterious understanding. My heart sparked. When next I saw her, I asked if she would like to attend a classical music concert with me the following Friday afternoon at the Cairo Opera House. She accepted and it became a regular outing for us even though neither of us really liked classical music. But it was a nice place to see each other away from campus life. What I felt for Amira was a tender affection, which I consider far more lasting than passionate love. Love harbors within it hate, and I could never hate Amira. Years have gone by since that first date and I sometimes wonder how our lives would have turned out had fate not sent us in different directions. To this day, I feel she is a part of me even though she is now married and a mother.

Twenty-one days before leaving Cairo for Qena, I came home to find that my uncle Fayid had collapsed from heat stroke. Despite the running fan to cool things down, the temperature was intolerable in the top-floor apartment where we lived. Everyone was on edge sharing a cramped space. The apartment had only two bedrooms, a small living room, and a tiny kitchen and bathroom. My uncle and his wife Nisma had their own room; the children and I shared the second one. My uncle was, of course, duty bound to put me up, but I sensed all along that Nisma resented my presence. She could say nothing, but acted in ways that reflected her frustration, taking it out on the children since it would have been rude to take it out on me. One day, for example, she sent them to the roof without lunch. She shouted that this was their punishment for talking back. It was a hot day and I felt responsible for the children's misery. I could not tell their mother what to do, of course, but I knew what I must do. I packed my bag, left my uncle's, and went to stay with a friend. When I related this incident to Amira, she said, wisely: "A friend may be able to help you once or twice, Nader, but keep in mind that he may then evade your company if he feels put upon. You could lose a friend in this way and also have your feelings hurt. Be careful." Was the transfer to Qena a blessing in disguise?

My friend Sayyed's father was a laborer with no education, but he was wise and often used proverbs to impart his wisdom. Two of his proverbs came to mind at this time. *Seeb li 'aduwwak wala teh tag li sadikak*, meaning, better to leave your wealth to an enemy than to be indebted to a friend. The other was, *humartak al 'argah wa la su'aal al la'eem*, meaning, better ride your own lame donkey than borrow a sturdy one from a cunning person, implying that if you do borrow from such a person you will forever be at his mercy.

Amira and I were sad at parting, but I hoped that by bettering myself, I could possibly one day win her hand. Even though there had been no declaration of love between us, we had a special bond and we promised to stay in touch. On one of my leaves to Cairo, I sought her out and was surprised when she told me that her mother was pressuring her to marry. She said that a number of suitors had come forward. It was her way of letting me know there was no time to lose. But what could I do? I asked her. She suggested I come to Alexandria to meet her parents. Of course, I could not. I had nothing to offer her yet. When I told her so, she was disappointed. When I said goodbye, she suggested that wherever we were we could listen to Um Kulthum at the same time on the first Thursday of every month and think of each other. I agreed, and before the next concert she clipped one of the songs published in the newspaper and sent it to me. I wrote back, but heard nothing more from Amira.

When I returned to Cairo on leave, I went to the college to see if I could find her. She was not there, but her friend Nagla told me that her family had taken her back to Alexandria because she had suffered a nervous breakdown. I was very sad to hear this but did not feel there was anything I could do, nor did I feel guilty. How can you regret something you are helpless to do anything about? If I have in my hand a glass of tea and you are thirsty and I don't give it to you, then I should feel regret and guilt at having failed you. But if I have neither tea, nor sugar, nor even water with which to make tea, I cannot offer you what I haven't got. In such an instance, I have not failed you.

Qena was a long train ride away, especially on the slow train, which I took because it was 1 Egyptian pound cheaper than the express. The trip took between 20 and 24 hours. The cars were creaky and decrepit, the windows were jammed open or shut. Passengers froze in winter, fried in summer, and all were covered in dust when they reached their destination. This train was called the sweeper, *al ashaash*, because it stopped at every village and hamlet from Cairo to Aswan. A single track ran between Aswan and Assiut, which became a double track only between Assiut and Cairo. This caused dramatic delays. Other trains always took priority over *al ashaash*, and if there was an accident or a repair being made on the track, you never knew when you might reach your destination.

After my leave ended, I boarded the train with plenty of time to get to Qena at daybreak, stop off at home to wash and change my clothes, and report to work promptly. But the *ashshaah* was being a slug as usual, inching its way south and arriving late, thus living up to its reputation. I had nicknamed this poor man's train *Laka'a Laka'a*, meaning "Lazy Bones," and memorized the rhythm of its trajectory: Go, creep, go, jerk, go, creep, creep, stop. Go, creep, go, jerk, go, creep, creep, stop. Creeeep creeeep, creeeep, creeeep jerk, creep, stop, and so on. We pulled into the station at 7 o'clock that Monday morning, a half hour before I was expected back on duty at the hospital. I went directly there, taking a few minutes to wash my face and tidy up as best I could in the staff room. The Qena Fever Hospital was an attractive structure, built in the Pharaonic style. The building was surrounded by spacious, well-kept grounds and a flower garden at the entrance planted with marigolds, daisies, and all sorts of other colorful varieties. It looked more like a five-star hotel than a hospital. The city of Qena itself was not so pleasant, its climate harsh, its people touchy. Winter was bitingly cold and summer so hot you could fry an egg in the sun in seconds. Qenawis were an envious, hot tempered, and devious lot, determined to undermine anyone with an edge. They did not like to see anyone better themselves and, in this environment, I had to be watchful or founder.

At the hospital, I was the number-two man. Along with the doctors on staff, I was the only civil servant. Others were local hires: nurses, housekeepers, cooks, groundskeepers, and the tall Sudanese gate keeper, looking like a king in his immaculate white *galabeyya*, or cotton kaftan, with wide sleeves and open neck. My duties were assigning work shifts, controlling hospital cleanliness, supervising menus, keeping records of stock in the storerooms, dispensing supplies, organizing visiting hours, working with the hospital accountant, writing daily progress reports, and admitting and discharging patients on doctors' orders.

The hospital did not provide my housing and therefore when I arrived in Qena, after a first night in the hotel, I was introduced to a group of young men at the coffee house. They invited me to share an apartment and I agreed. One of the housemates was a poet who later became an Egyptian icon; the others were all students. Quickly I realized the arrangement would not work for me and began to look for another place to live. Personalities were not compatible, my housemates found me too serious, and I was often the butt of jokes and jibes such as, "What are you going to do with a law degree?" My salary was under 10 Egyptian pounds per month and the rent and utilities were too high if I wanted anything left over for books, or trips back to Cairo to sit for my exams, and my new habit, cigarettes. I bought my first pack in Qena on my first night there when, feeling dejected, I went out for a walk to clear my head and think. I had taken a drink at the bar and realized alcohol would be my undoing if I was not vigilant. I watched Qenawis go into the bar in the morning, drink cheap brandy, wine, and arak all day until, by midnight, the town was full of drunks. I determined never to go in that place again. I kept my eyes on the goals I had set for myself and this is what saved me.

After a month of shared housing, I gave notice and rented a small ground-floor room in an old apartment building. A shared bathroom was on a square courtyard at the back of the building. There too a cold water spigot served me and the family of the *bawaab*, the doorkeeper whose duty it was to sweep and keep the building in order and collect the rent for the landlord. The room was dark and airless, but I figured that I was gone all day and would not find it too oppressive. The rent was 1 Egyptian pound a month, just right. I decided to create a kitchen nook into which I installed an oil lamp, an alcohol burner, a small teapot and a canister with tea and sugar, a spoon, and a knife. Sometimes I bought fruit, a cucumber, or a handful of peanuts for a snack, but I ate most of my meals at the hospital. My room had a dirt floor. I had to be careful of scorpions, which are the curse of Qena. I never put my shoes on without first shaking them and likewise my clothing. I bought a narrow metal bed and mattress, two pillows, a blanket and quilt from the department store Omar Effendi, and, very cheaply, from a local artisan who made palm-wood products, I bought a *gareed* table and chair, just right to sit and study or read my Qur'an by the light of my lamp. I stayed two years in this room, paying one of the hospital housekeepers to do my laundry so I would always be clean and well dressed. She was a godsend.

In my second month in Qena, I set a schedule for myself from which I rarely deviated. This kept me on an even keel. I rose in the morning with the call of the *mu'ezzin*: "*allahu akbar, allahu akbar, ashhadu anna la ilah illa allah, ashhadu anna muh-hamadan rasulul lah*" (God is great, God is great, I bear witness that there is no God but God, I bear witness that Muhammad is God's messenger). I performed my ablutions according to *surat al maida*, "O believers, when you rise up to prayer, wash your faces and your hands to the elbows, wipe your heads and your feet to the ankles . . . ," then I then prayed *al fajr* (at dawn), dressed, and, at 7 o'clock, walked to the hospital. At the hospital I had my first cup of coffee and another *mazbut* (sugared just right) at 10 o'clock. I performed my duties until noon and studied at my desk from noon until 2 o'clock when Dr. Rafik came in to update me on patients before going home for his lunch. I ate mine at the hospital, then took a nap at 3 o'clock in the staff rest room, which had a couple of white metal beds. I woke promptly at 5 o'clock, had a glass of tea, made my last rounds of the day, checked on schedules, updated the staff coming in for night duty, wrote my daily reports, and went home. At home, I washed at the spigot in the courtyard, changed, lit my lamp, made a glass of tea, and settled back down to study for the rest of the evening. Before retiring for the night, I took a walk, returned home, performed my ablutions and prayed *al-'isha* (dusk to before midnight prayers), and at 12 o'clock blew out my lamp and went to bed. There was no room for backsliding. Discipline and my faith in God's mercy gave me the strength to carry on.

Many of my coworkers were a conniving bunch and hated to see me improve my lot. I'll tell you one of the stories of how, time and time again, they looked for ways to defeat me. One day, an Englishman was brought to the hospital. He was very sick and the doctor diagnosed him with typhoid fever. He had been hitchhiking from the Sudan to Egypt and, upon reaching Qena, was found collapsed on the street and placed under quarantine. He fled, then was apprehended in the town of Dishna, brought back to Qena, and again quarantined. This incident took place on the eve of my leave. I had tickets to catch the train to Cairo the next day and had quit early to prepare for my trip. I was not in the hospital when the English patient was brought in. One of the staff reported that I had been at the hospital and had been in contact with the patient. Just as I reached the train station and got ready to board the 9 o'clock train, a messenger from the hospital ran up huffing and puffing and told me I was ordered to return to the hospital. I asked him why and he told me. I instructed him then to go back to the hospital and say he had not found me. I did not want him to be penalized for not bringing me in, but I knew that he knew that the person who had reported my contact with the patient was lying. He had a vested interest in retaining my favor, as I had the power to move him to a job with no contact with the public instead of the one he held that allowed him contact with patients. Over and above his meager salary he received significant tips and gratuities for his services from the families of the patients. This is an example of the mischief I encountered as well as the power a hospital superintendent can misuse.

When I returned from Cairo, I met the Englishman and we became friends. I did my best to make him comfortable, knowing how hard it must have been for him to be sick and away from home. I taught him a little Arabic, he taught me a little English; I had special food prepared for him, brought him chocolate bars a few times when he had begun to feel better. He recovered, went home, got married, and returned to Egypt with his bride. They came to see me and I still have a photo of the two of them taken with me at the time of their visit.

In my second year at the Qena Fever Hospital, I learned another lesson I would never forget, as it nearly brought about the collapse of everything I had worked for. We received a call at the hospital that some documents were needed at the Ministry of Health. Someone had to go to Cairo to take them and bring them back. I could earn an extra 10 Egyptian pounds if I took the assignment. I jumped at the chance, but did not have the extra 2 pounds for the express train that I had to take to get to Cairo with dispatch. The 10 pounds would be paid only upon my return. I reasoned that it was now the 27th of the month, just a few days short of my payday, and if I borrowed the 2 pounds from the hospital safe, I could promptly repay it on my return.

When I got to Cairo, however, I was told to turn back and to tell the "gentlemen of Qena" that "the gentlemen from the ministry" found their paperwork shoddy and incomplete and that they would not accept it. "Take it back and have it filled it out properly," they commanded. This was typical of the bureaucracy we had to deal with almost on a daily basis. I returned to Qena empty-handed and found myself in a jam, as the accounts supervisor had picked that day to "control" the safe. I was short 2 pounds and two days short of payday. What to do? If he had already audited the books, he would have found the discrepancy. I excused myself, saying I was just going to freshen up after my trip and return to help him. Instead, I ran for help to my friend Dr. Nakhla, may God bless him. I explained my predicament and he loaned me the money, which I returned to the safe thinking no one was the wiser. I subsequently found out that the supervisor had noticed the missing 2 pounds but decided not to report it until he had spoken to me. He, Dr. Nakhla, and Dr. Rafik knew my reputation and were among the few friends I had in Qena. When the money was discovered back in the safe, Dr. Rafik spared me the embarrassment of a confrontation. I vowed that I would never again make such a foolish mistake.

In my second year at the hospital, I applied for holiday leave to go home to Qutur. I had not seen my parents or my siblings in a year and was longing to be with my family. In preparation for the feast, I went to a tailor and had a new suit made. I had saved some money from my salary, as my rent was cheap and my expenses minimal. The suit cost 12 Egyptian pounds for the wool and the tailoring, and the tailor agreed to let me pay him in installments of 1 pound a month for a year. I was so proud of my new suit and felt so good wearing it. I had chosen a lightweight wool, a dark coffee color with a lighter pin stripe. I wore brown shoes polished to a high sheen and a dark tie with flecks of red in it. I remember it all so well and to this day it remains my favorite outfit, probably because it was the first thing I bought myself and it was hard earned. I looked sharp and the thought crossed my mind that not even the president of the United States of America could have a better suit! I boarded the train, and when I got to Tanta, I ran into one of the nurses from Qena. I greeted her and offered her a glass of tea at the canteen while we waited for our connections. When the time came, I walked her to her train and wished her a safe journey and happy feast. Little did I know that this act of courtesy would have consequences for me, but I continued to Qutur where my parents eagerly awaited me. When I arrived home, my mother ululated with joy and I offered her a 10-pound note, money I had saved.

My father gave me his wedding ring when I first left for Qena, saying I should wear it for protection. He knew the world better than I did, and was apprehensive that some female at the hospital would try to entrap me. As it turned out, he was right. He asked about my trip and I told him in passing that I had run into a nurse from the Qena hospital in Tanta and walked her to her train after a glass of tea together. My father suddenly looked alarmed and said to me, "Nader, my son, keep your eyes open, nurses are a shady lot!" He told me to keep the ring on and pretend that I had a wife at home. So I did, and when I returned to Qena my coworkers met me with words of congratulations: "*Mabruk, mabruk*" (Blessings, blessings)! I was surprised at such enthusiasm about my new suit, for this is what I thought they were referring to. What an innocent I was! I answered politely, "*Allah ye barek fikum*" (And may God bless you), but then I noticed them eyeing the ring on my finger. It was not until Dr. Nakhla burst into my office that all was finally made clear. He brought his fist down on my desk and said, "What have you done, you fool? Have you taken leave of your senses?!"

As it turned out, a rumor had been circulated that I was engaged to be married to the nurse I met in Tanta and that the ring on my finger was an engagement ring. The nurse had put a ring on her finger as well, which led everyone to believe the rumor. Someone said later that it was meant as a joke, but it was no joke to me. I had to find a way to extricate myself. I did not want to discredit and embarrass the nurse in public by saying she was a liar, so I let a few days go by and then confronted her: "Look Abla Safiyya, I don't want to hurt or discredit you nor do I wish for you to lose face but this game must stop now. Go tell your colleagues that we have broken our engagement and we can forget this whole charade!" I did not wait for her reply. I had given her a way out without embarrassment and she knew it. She did as I asked and the incident was dismissed as a prank even though it could have had dire consequences. Such webs of intrigue and depravity are ever lurking among us and for this reason I unfailingly invoke God's protection, often reciting the last *sura* from the holy Qur'an, *surat an naas* (of mankind): "*Bismillah al Rahman al Raheem*, In the name of God the merciful, say: I seek refuge with the Lord of mankind, the King of mankind, the real God of mankind, I seek refuge from the evil of the whisperer (*Al Wiswaas Al Khannaas*) be he man or Jinn (spirit being) who whispers [evil thoughts] into the hearts of men."

Nurses in Egypt have, alas, earned a bad reputation. In their defense, I must say that often their actions are motivated by the predicament they find themselves in. They are needed yet not respected, and a boy or girl from a middle-class or upper-class family would never wish to be found in their shoes. No "good" family would allow one of its members to join this professing. So I will say that until this taboo is broken, until nurses and the nursing profession are viewed with respect, nothing will change. Would the son of a respectable family be allowed to marry a nurse today? You can guess the answer. Young interns came to

Qena Fever Hospital and other hospitals with little experience of mixing with the opposite sex and found themselves entrapped. Imagine a young man away from home and lonely. He finds himself in a training hospital in the provinces, living at close quarters with females. He does all the wrong things. Or, imagine a girl who works in close quarters with a doctor who declares that he loves her. She is bound to weaken and fall in love with him. He, of course, has no intention of marrying her, but she is dreaming of becoming a doctor's wife. She puffs out with pride and when her hopes are dashed she thinks of revenge.

While in Qena, I witnessed this scene: A nurse came shrieking into the men's staff room, her clothes torn and her face scratched, and cried, "Help!" She got the attention of the staff, and the young doctor had to marry her. They were both victims, actually. What a backward social system! I thought, "I could have been this young intern!" I resolved to be cautious, but meanwhile a cousin came to Qena who was a busybody and a troublemaker. He had been let out of prison, where he served some years for his activities in the Muslim Brotherhood movement. He called on me at the hospital and saw my ring. He took it upon himself to tell my father that I had married a nurse. I tried to avoid him, but he clung to me and continued to cause trouble. Although my father knew about the ring and he and I did not keep secrets from each other, he worried when he heard the rumor. Now that I was employed and living on my own, father treated me like an equal, but there were a few things I never did in his presence, like crossing my legs while sitting or smoking. These are small courtesies, but in our culture they signify to an elder or a superior that we respect them.

My father's concern grew despite my reassurances and he dispatched Abu Sayyid to check on me. Abu Sayyid traveled free of charge on the trains because he was a railway employee. I was surprised and pleased when he turned up at the hospital and

ordered lunch for him, but he declined and asked to go home
with me instead. I sent him ahead, suggesting he rest from his
trip until I finished my duties and could join him. I brought
lunch, headed home, and was surprised to find Abu Sayyid rum-
maging through my things: "Is something wrong, Abu Sayyid?
You seem to be searching for something." He answered, "Look
here, son, you are just as dear to me as my son Sayyid. I can't
keep anything from you. Your cousin sent word to your father
that you had married a nurse. Your father sent me to find out. I
was looking for evidence of a woman in the house, but I have not
found any." Why didn't my father confront me himself? Perhaps
he felt responsible for my ending up in Qena. Had he been able
to support me, I would still be in Cairo, studying full time at Ayn
Shams. But if I had married, the deed was done and he did not
wish to alienate me. It was the only reason I could think of for
his behavior. I was angry and sent a letter back with Abu Sayyid
that I later regretted, and I did not go back to Qutur for a year.
Time dispels anger, however. I returned, kissed my father's head
in apology, and we were friends again.

One day I felt a sharp pain on my right side. I went to see my
friend Dr. Mitri at the Amiri Hospital. He examined me and said,
"You have appendicitis. Check yourself into the hospital and I'll
operate on you tomorrow at 8." That evening, he came back to
jolly me along. A well-meaning or meddlesome staff member,
knowing I had a cousin in town, called the fellow, who came,
bringing with him a surgeon friend from the Amiri Hospital.
They were both members of the Muslim Brotherhood. He told
me he would do the surgery, perhaps imagining that I would prefer him, a Muslim, to Dr. Mitri, a Christian. He was mistaken.
I knew each doctor's reputation and happened to know that
this one was a brute. He took shortcuts, made large incisions,
was insensitive to patients. It was late, but I called Dr. Mitri,
who said, "Relax, Nader, we'll operate at 4 in the morning." He

rescheduled and, true to his word, arrived promptly to perform the surgery before the other surgeon arrived. Although this is a simple-enough operation, I had an unusual reaction to the anesthetic, given by injection into the spine. I didn't get numb, and when I finally did, I didn't stay numb. I heard Dr. Mitri ask for clamps, and then I felt a sharp pain and said, "I feel the clamps, doctor," and passed out. Dr. Mitri told me my heart had stopped for 30 seconds. When I came to, I saw my gentle surgeon's worried face covered in sweat. I asked him to change the intravenous needle to the other arm, and when he heard my voice, he smiled in relief and teased, "Nader, you have not been brave!" And after this, everything was fine until the other doctor came and proceeded to yank off my bandage, saying, "So you went behind my back, did you? Let me check this out!" Yank! I was shocked. I was twenty, not much more than a boy caught in a cross fire fueled by prejudice and stupidity. I saw the face of mean-spiritedness and pettiness in this man who called himself pious, and came to despise the bigotry that motivated him and others like him. He was so much like Qena itself! As to that cousin, thank God I never saw him again.

I was sitting in my office one day, the door open, screen shut to keep out insects, a breeze bringing a hint of relief from the heat of the day. I had finished my evening rounds when I heard a gunshot. I knew of the feuding that went on between the *Hamdat*, the *Hawara*, and the *Ashraf* clans of Qena. Why were they killing one another? Some of the reasons had been buried in the sands of time. One, however, had to do with the patron saint of Qena, Abd al Rahim al Kenaawi. The *Hamdans* claimed to be direct descendants, whereas the *Hawara* said they were even more closely related to the saintly man. Both vied for the privilege of conducting the festivities for his birthday, his *mulid*, including the privilege of placing an elaborate ritual covering over his tomb. Finally, in the 1950s, the government directed the elected governor of the province to do the honors, taking it out of the hands of the clans, who were told the feast would be banned if they did not comply. The clans made a show of peace, but like so much else in Upper Egypt it was not clear what was brewing under the surface.

Summer came and the town was bursting with officials, police, locals, and visitors come to celebrate the mulid. Shaykh Abd al Basit Abd al Samat, a Qur'anic chanter and a native of Qena who was at the time at the height of his fame, was in attendance. The feast lasted several days. All went well until the last night when everyone proceeded across the railroad tracks to the mosque and tomb of Sidi Abd al Rahim. A freight train was blocking the way. The governor and his guests were there, accompanied by a motorcade with sirens and the usual ceremonies. A huge crowd followed. The governor decided that the officials and VIPs should get out of their cars and walk across. The crowd jostled each other, broke into the midst of the delegation, and chaos ensued. The police swung their clubs into the crowd and people panicked and stampeded. Seventy people died and three hundred were badly injured. Upper Egyptians are famous for their hot tempers and feuds. The incident in Qena was an example and made national headlines.

In neighboring Dishna, also known as al Samata, such an incident took place in 1960. Police had arrested a villager, who died while in their custody. Men, women, and children of his village and fourteen other villages laid siege to police headquarters for three days and established the Independent Republic of Dishna. Zakariyya Mohieddin, then minister of the interior, declared it a national emergency and sent troops to the area to break up the siege. Tanks and armed troops passed right in front of the hospital on their way to Dishna and we could hear gunshot 45 kilometers away, echoing off the mountains west of Qena. A relic of that time, a tank, stands in front of the Qena police headquarters to this day, a reminder of Dishna's brief secession. So it goes in the south of Egypt, in Upper Egypt.

From the first, the governor of Qena and Dr. Rafik did not see eye to eye. Tensions increased with time, and it was in the course of a conflict between them that I was able to show my loyalty to Dr. Rafik. Qena Fever Hospital was known as a model hospital, and when the governor wanted to impress visitors, he brought them here. We ran a tight ship and schedules were kept. At 7 in the morning I was on the job. At 7:30 the staff attendance book was removed and replaced by one for latecomers. A half hour later, the gates were closed and locked until visiting hours. Dr. Amgad, the chief resident, was an excellent doctor, compassionate and an excellent diagnostician. If he thought that a patient was nearing death, he alerted me and I did what I could for the patient and the family. He did not trust the nurses to give patients medication and did it himself, even if he had to return to the hospital or stay there all night. Often I'd find him at a patient's bedside early in the morning. He would say: "Now that you're here, I'll go get some sleep in the doctors' lounge, Nader. Wake me for up for medications." One day, however, Dr. Amgad went home sick and the nurses were to give the medications. He instructed me to make sure they did. His routine was to check empty vials and bottles against stock in the dispensary and make sure all was in order.

On one fateful morning, the governor arrived before Dr. Amgad. He found all of the used vials piled on a table and began to shout. I explained that this was not neglect but that it was a way of keeping count, but he accused me of trying to cover up for the doctor. I said, "Dr. Amgad will be here shortly, Your Excellency, and he can show you that all medications are under lock and key at the pharmacy. These are the empties used to control what he has dispensed." Eventually the governor was impressed by what he saw and gave a 10-pound bonus to each member of the staff. When Dr. Rafik heard of this, he thanked me. He knew the governor wanted to get rid of him and that on this surprise visit he was looking for discrepancies.

All was well for a while, but the day came when the governor did get rid of Dr. Rafik on some trumped-up charge. No one from the hospital dared go to the train station with him, fearing they too would be targeted. I did, and Dr. Rafik thanked me for my loyalty. Before he boarded, he said, "Good luck, Nader. Don't think I ever had anything against you personally," and was gone.

During my third year in Qena I missed Dr. Rafik. The intrigue at the hospital escalated and I decided I had to leave. I put in for a transfer and was assigned to Esna, which was 3 hours farther south and would mean a cut in salary, 12 pounds a month instead of the 14 I was earning. Never mind, I thought, I had to get out and did not hesitate. I must say that the doctors encouraged me and I left with no regret. I said goodbye, gathered my belongings, returned the key of the room to the *bawaab*, boarded the morning train going south, and arrived in Esna at noon of the same day.

Esna was a small, friendly town. People invited newcomers to their homes. The staff and town officials were kind and helpful, the people I came in contact with were interested in what I was doing and encouraged me to continue my studies. After work, a bunch of us got together to socialize, including the hospital director, public prosecutor, police chief, and a variety of businessmen. We went for walks along the Esna bridge, enjoying that beautiful stretch of river, stopping for tea at a local cafe. No women were involved. There was an apartment associated with the job waiting for me in Esna, but the rent was too high. Tarek Salem, a colleague, invited me to share his apartment and I accepted. It was airy and pleasant on the top floor of a small building overlooking the Nile. We each had a bedroom and shared a bath and the kitchen. He did the shopping and

I did the cooking and we got along as if we had been friends of long-standing. The bedrooms had no doors and faced each other across a small living room where we had set up a table and two chairs by the window. Often at night we chatted across the living room before saying goodnight, *tisbah a la khayr*, may you sleep and rise in good health. Each of us paid 1 Egyptian pound rent per month and 25 piasters for utilities. It was ideal and I was happy.

The nurses at Esna were a decent bunch and often when they cooked meals for themselves, they included me and also offered to do my laundry. I was grateful, and the relationships I developed were cordial and reminded me a little of the brotherliness and sisterliness I had with my friends in Qutur. The nurses had their own residence on the hospital grounds and had their own kitchen. One, Satuta, nicknamed *Susta* (spring) because she had a spring to her step, was famous for her *kushari* and when she made it she always saved me a portion.

One day Satuta introduced me to a young woman named Huda, a visiting trainee health inspector from Cairo who stopped by to see me a week or two later and asked if I could help her obtain a pass to go on leave on a family matter. I went to see the hospital director and he granted it. When she returned from Cairo she came to see me in my office and thanked me. Every now and again she stopped to say hello or have a glass of tea. I became interested in Huda and began to think of marriage. After I passed my law finals and received my degree, I would be ready to settle down. Huda was the right sort of girl. She came from a good family, was nice looking, intelligent, pleasantly conversant. And, above all, she did not seem to object to my attentions, so I began to court her. When I asked for her parents' address in Cairo, she gave it to me, and I wrote to them and got a letter back from one of her brothers. Huda had told them about me, he said, and they would be glad to meet me when I came to Cairo. As there were no family members in Esna to keep an eye on us or to chaperone, her brother appealed to my sense of honor and said, "I am entrusting my sister to your care, Nader," a way to make sure I would treat her with respect, like a sister.

When I went home to Qutur over the holidays and told my father that I had met someone I would like to marry, he asked: "What is her name?" I said, "Huda." He asked: "Huda who?" I said, "Huda 'Allaam." He asked: "Where does her father live?" I told him, adding, "She has two brothers, one an engineer and one a teacher, and a cousin who is secretary to the minister of the interior." There was a thoughtful pause, then my father said, "You know, Nader, this family is related to your mother. The son of your mother's maternal uncle is married to Huda's paternal aunt." I replied, "How lucky. That means we know who they are." My father hesitated. I asked, "Is anything wrong?" He said, haltingly: "No, no, nothing," instead of "congratulations" or words of that nature. He seemed uncomfortable and I wondered what was on his mind but said nothing, nor did he.

I went back to Esna and Huda and I put in for transfers to Cairo. We took the train to Luxor and went shopping for jewelry, the *shabka* for her, something she would like, which would seal our engagement. Traditionally it would have been a gold bracelet, perhaps in the form of a snake, turquoise studded, or a gold chain and pendant, or a necklace and earrings, an engagement ring, or even a wedding ring. She chose a gold filigree necklace, matching earrings and ring, and soon after we returned together to Cairo where our families had arranged to meet and celebrate our engagement. In their presence, I offered Huda the *shabka* she herself had picked, and she wore it. We were happy, or so we thought. A cousin suggested we print a wedding announcement. To my astonishment, Huda's mother snapped, "And whom can we say my daughter is marrying? A hospital superintendent?!" My father stiffened. I felt as if I had been slapped. My father came to my aid and, alluding to one of her kin, said to her: "My son is a university graduate, Madame. His law degree is one he earned with his own sweat and blood, unlike some who pay for theirs!" I realized then how closely my father had lived my struggle and how seriously he took this damaging remark. Huda's mother came from a relatively wealthy family and, even though her family's lands had been seized and nationalized after the revolution, she was arrogant. She had the fair good looks of women of Turkish origin, who consider themselves a cut above Egyptians with Egyptian roots. It was clear she would remind me every chance she got that I was marrying up. I was too proud to back out now and too smitten with Huda or the idea of Huda, perhaps, to give her up even though in my heart of hearts I knew I was not in love and knew her mother would make it hard for us. However, what I saw was an attractive young woman from a good family who would look good as the wife of a young man newly graduated from law school and all puffed up with ambition. Yes, that was me. What I imagined was a union that was mutually beneficial and children who benefitted from being raised by two educated parents in the heart of two families, one from the country, the other from the city, and that they would have the best of both worlds. I reasoned too that Huda and I would find a way to make it a good marriage, as we were both ready to start a family. I did not give adequate credence to the little voice within that was saying, "Don't do it." I reasoned that if we ran into difficulty (part of life, I said to myself) we would talk them through and smooth them out. I could not have been more wrong.

On the first day of the feast of Ramadan, I went to Qutur and brought back my youngest sister to celebrate with us in Cairo. I had bought a gold ring for Huda and so got one for my sister too as a token of affection. When we got to Huda's parents' home, it was gloomy and Huda had been crying. Her sister-in-law, Rahma, took me aside and said, "Mother wants you to sign the marriage contract right now or take back your gifts," meaning, break the engagement. She was twisting my arm, trying to get me to back out although we had previously agreed that the engagement would be for one full year so Huda and I could get to know each other and also to give me a chance to better prepare myself financially. Huda's mother couldn't break the engagement herself without losing face, so she used every ploy she could think of to force me to do it. Rahma liked me and took me aside and said: "She wants Huda to marry her sister's son and that's why she can't wait to get you out of the way." Everything about this situation indicated trouble ahead, but I stubbornly plowed on convincing myself that I was actually falling in love with Huda and she with me.

I am proud and stubborn, and this stubborn streak sees me through many difficulties when it is transformed into perseverance. However, in the case of Huda and her family, it caused me nothing but embarrassment and heartache. Even when I was a child I was stubborn. I remember an incident in Qutur when my mother and aunt were cleaning, I opened doors and windows and the cross-draft picked up dust and scattered it all over. My mother reprimanded me and told me to get out from underfoot. I pushed the shutters wider and screamed when my fingers got pinched between them. When my father got home, he took my side, blaming my mother and aunt for being careless and not watching out for me. He was wrong, of course, but his validation of what I had done added mortar to my stubborn nature. I was used to succeeding, but this has also been the cause of some misguided decisions I have made. We each have our destiny and we follow along and cannot always take credit or blame for what happens to us. At times, however, we can be our own worst enemy.

I would like to tell you a little about Egyptian women. The Egyptian woman never speaks her mind when it comes to feelings. She plays a game of hide and seek, hoping the man will understand what she wants or what she wants of him. She wants to be loved and yet resists tenderness for fear of appearing weak. A misplaced word or one that she considers wounding or negative can cause a host of problems to rain down on a marriage. If a man is richer than his wife, he may look down on her and by his tone make her feel he has honored her by marrying her. Say he is a professor and she a social worker, she may not be able to keep up with him intellectually or socially. This creates a fissure in their marriage. If there is little love, understanding, or compassion, such situations can bring the house down around a couple's heads. Ideally, an intelligent woman can bridge many gaps and by acting wisely. By overlooking certain differences by skirting negative family pressures, she can save her marriage. She can go shoulder to shoulder with her husband as he moves up. A man needs a woman to watch over him, to guide him, to share in his decision making. His wife must have reached a level of understanding that permits her to be his helpmate. Some gaps are too wide, however. Sadly, the middle-class Egyptian woman's ambition is to get married, have children, and bicker with her husband. This is how the majority views marriage. Huda and I fell into this category. Here's a typical scenario. A wife goes to work dressed to kill, her hair coiffed by the hairdresser, her makeup carefully applied. At the office, she smiles, laughs, jokes with her colleagues, orders tea from the janitor or a cold drink for a visitor stopping to chat at her desk. She exchanges news and views and at 1 o'clock, as the offices are about to close, she undergoes a total transformation. Suddenly she has a headache, her arthritis has flared up or her knees are sore. A litany of complaints rises out of her desk drawers, replacing the smile that she pushes deep into her purse, snapping it shut. Imagine meeting a frowning wife every day of your life as you get home? True, she is as tired as you are because like you she works. You, the husband, should be considerate. You should get up and get your own tea or water. You should help out. In all fairness, I must say that few Egyptian husbands are helpful in the home. Complaining becomes a lifestyle for many middle-class women. She cannot openly seek or admit that what she wants is her husband's attention. So she beats around the bush. Little do most couples know that the problem is not the illnesses and discomforts themselves, but that they are the mask behind which the problems hide. When there is little or no communication, marriage becomes a desert. It became a desert for Huda and me, and by the time we were ready to stop fighting and admit that the marriage was not going to work, we had two daughters. Eventually there was nothing for it but divorce. And so we divorced.

I think for us both, divorce was the right step. Once I made up my mind, nothing could stop me. People said, "Think of the children, people disagree all the time, this is life," etc. My answer was, "If I've been unjust to her, then I am unwilling to have her suffer more at my hands. I cannot change. If she has been unjust, I will not put up with it any longer." We assumed responsibility for the mistakes we made. She believed in the precept, weigh him down with kids and keep his pockets empty and he'll never be able to leave, because she could not escape what she had been taught. I could not tolerate a loveless marriage where bickering and discord were the daily bread. People think sex is the deal breaker, but I am convinced that lack of desire is the tip of the iceberg. Why does a couple's sexual desire for each other fade? Well, consider this. When the wife says, "He's neglecting me," she is expressing the consequence of a long line of problems. Neglect is not the opening chapter. Look at a banana tree: the fruit is the result of how well you care for the tree. A cat when you pet it will cuddle you or conversely scratch you if you mistreat it. Or if constantly you push it away, it will stop coming to you. So it is with us humans. When there is compassion between a man and a woman, forgiveness for weaknesses or faults, affectionate conversation, trust, a way of being together that promotes comfort and security, then love flourishes and in its wake sexual desire is born. I assure you, it is not the other way around!

When Huda and I divorced, I said to the girls: "If you wish to stay with your mother, I'll leave the house. If you wish to stay with me, then she should leave." They were teenagers and chose to stay with me. I have raised them tenderly, protected them, yet respected their freedom, needs, and wishes. I see before me two young women who, I hope, will not make the same mistakes their mother and I made and who will lead happy and fulfilling lives, remembering that faith in God sustains us at all times and in every circumstance.

I consider my life an interesting life. My childhood years were the happiest years and my daughters are my greatest gift. I have accomplished much of what I set out to accomplish and can now reap the benefits of my efforts. This is my story until now. I am grateful to get up in the morning, I am grateful for all that I have experienced, and I thank God for his mercy. *Al hamdu 'l illah!*

Nader Bestawros

My mother's name is Demiana Habib. My father was Daoud Bestawros. In Egypt, women keep their maiden name after they marry. My parents were cousins, related through their mothers, which is why their last names are different. They were born and raised in Assiut in a largely Christian neighborhood of this Upper Egypt city. They lived in other cities too, but their roots were in Assiut and in the nearby family village of Ashmunayn, also in the south of Egypt, which we call *al Saeed*.

My parents were born into a traditional Coptic family. The Coptic Church is an ancient and venerable church, the monophysite Christian church of Egypt. The Egyptians were converted to Christianity by Saint Mark, who came to Alexandria in AD 42. From the third century, Christianity spread through rural Egypt until the seventh century, when the Arabs conquered Egypt and forced Christians to convert to Islam on pain of death or a steep tax. You will see as I tell you my story that my parents never relinquished a firm grip on their Christian faith, although my father abandoned the Coptic Church. He was persuaded by missionaries to join the Plymouth Brothers, a Protestant sect proselytizing in Egypt, especially in Upper Egypt. My mother held fast to the Coptic Church, however, her affection for it never waning. This was a source of discord between my parents. But that is a story for later.

After my parents were married they lived in Cairo for a time and then moved back to Assiut just before their first child was born. They rented an airy apartment on the top floor of a building erected in the early 1900s. My father refused to live anywhere but on the top floor of any building. He said he did not wish to see his wife or daughters "wounded" by an untoward glance or word from any man, or from any strangers, neighbors, or anyone going up the stairs or coming down the stairs past their apartment door. Nor, said he, would he allow them to be exposed to the same when they sat on their balconies. Theirs had to be the top-floor balcony that looked down on other balconies. Of course the rooftop was above, but this was the domain of women who went there to wash or to gather dry laundry from laundry lines at the end of the day. If it was not the women of the house doing the laundry, it would be a washerwoman. It was understood that men did not go up to the roof, at least not where we lived.

In this apartment building where father and mother raised their family for a time, there was one apartment to each floor and a spacious, north-facing balcony overlooking the street. A small green area with grass and trees formed a triangular median that was maintained by the city. A man came twice a month, scythe in hand, to cut the grass and collect leaves and weeds in a woven basket that he dumped on his handcart and hauled away.

On summer evenings we sat on the balcony enjoying the cooling of the day and the breezes. The warm season lasted from May through September, when temperatures could reach 100 degrees Fahrenheit. Winter was from December through February, with average temperatures in the 70s, dipping down to the 40s at times. So in winter, the balcony was the nicest place to sit to warm ourselves in the sun. During the warmer part of the day mother aired the rooms and sat on the balcony to enjoy the sun and do whatever little chores she had on hand. After sunset, the shutters and windows were closed tight against the night chill.

As I child, I imagined the desert wind as a giant broom, sweeping the town cool in summer. In March and April, however, with the advent of the *khamsin* winds, that broom was frantic, sweeping sand and grit from the desert, which seeped under doors and windows and filled one's nostrils, ears, and hair. In Egypt, the desert is close to everywhere and we are affected by its moods. Years later, in the United States, I heard the saying, "March comes in like a lion and goes out like a lamb," and thought it an apt description of the *khamsin* winds.

Our apartment had three bedrooms, a large family room, and a parlor off to one side used for guests, which we referred to as the "salon" and also *odit al guloos* (literally, sitting room). We considered this room the showpiece of our home. It was crowded with gilded furniture: chairs in the Louis-sixteenth style so popular among the Egyptian middle classes to this day. There were two chairs and a love seat upholstered in dark-red velvet, two small square tables topped with marble, and a matching oval one decorated with a cloth my sister Sawsan had embroidered.

The kitchen was small and the bathroom had a high window for ventilation and a glass transom above the door. We had cold running water that we heated for bathing. When I was in high school, my parents bought and installed a butane water heater and we have not been without hot water since. The toilet was a water closet with a pull chain, which means that the water for flushing was in a tank above the commode, not directly attached to it.

The family room was square and had two divans and two Aswan chairs made of wood with wide arms; it could be reclined slightly by pulling a rod out of the back and placing it on a lower rung. Many a time I pinched my fingers playing with those chairs. They had removable cushions with gold-and-green-striped slipcovers and a table with a gold crocheted doily in between.

The dining room was right off the family room and had a big rectangular table, eight chairs, and a buffet where my mother kept glasses with pink rims, dishes, cutlery, and a white table-cloth with twelve matching napkins, all of it to set the table when we had company, which was only family around feast times. The ceilings were decorated with plaster moldings in the form of grape clusters and leaves. My mother, who was clever with her hands, had made crocheted panels with a pattern of grape clusters to go on each side of the window and above it. She had seen ones like them and liked them. She had memorized the design and copied it for our home.

The bedrooms were plain, except that my parent's bed had a headboard with angels on it and a matching armoire. The children's rooms had beds and desks.

The ceilings throughout the apartment were about 12-feet high, keeping it cool in summer but chilly in winter, as we had no heating and went outside to sit in the sun to warm up during the day. Mother would say to my sisters, *Yalla nit shammes*, "let's go out and sun ourselves." In summer we retreated indoors behind closed shutters. People joked that only fools and Englishmen went out in the midday sun!

Washing was done by hand, of course. A washerwoman was hired who remained with us for many years. Her name was Um Fadel, mother of Fadel, her firstborn son. Washing was heavy work and Um Fadel had the arms for it, the arms of a wrestler. She also had the gravelly voice of a smoker or someone who does a lot of shouting, which she did. Washerwomen had the reputation of being rough and a little coarse, something like "fishmongers" in other cultures. Um Fadel (Fadel being the laundress's son) insisted on calling my mother Um Nader, thus showing partiality to me, the son. My mother corrected her, saying that she was the mother of her firstborn, my sister Sawsan, and this banter was like a sort of comedy routine between them. My mother declared: *"Ana Um Sawsan, Y'um Fadel, Ana Um Sawsan"* (I am first Sawsan's, not Nader's, mother, Um Fadel)!

But Um Fadel persisted and never mended her ways. Mothers in Upper Egypt found status in being mothers of the preferred gender, the male. In this respect, my mother was different. She said, *Ana Um al banaat* (I am proud to be the mother of girls). This does not mean that she did not appreciate or love her sons, but I think she tried to balance the cultural preference for males by validating her daughters in this way. My father did not interfere. This was women's talk.

On washday, Um Fadel heated water on a parafin stove called a Primus, which sounded like a blowtorch when it was fired up. We also used it for cooking. You maintained it by cleaning soot buildup from the heads with a special tool that came with the stove. It was a small, flat piece of tin with a fine needle at the end of it. You also had to adjust the mechanism that pumped the fuel into the stove so it would run efficiently. It was a reliable little stove found in every Egyptian home until gas stoves became readily available. These were easier to use and for people who could afford them they were preferred. They came with portable butane gas tanks that were exchanged or refilled as needed. Poor families, however, still rely on the Primus.

Um Fadel hauled the washtub to the roof along with the square bar of yellow lye soap my mother allotted for the job. The washtub, called a *karawana*, was made of tin-washed copper that had to be re-tinned periodically. It was about a foot high and 3 feet or so in diameter. Whites were boiled, scrubbed, and kneaded by hand using the lye soap, then rinsed well and dried in the sun. Sometimes, *zahra* (blueing) was added to the rinse water to brighten the whites and gave them a slight lavender tinge.

The drying lines were strung from one end of the roof to the other, the laundry secured with wooden pegs called *mashaabek*. Every family had their own stove, tub, and pins. The wash had to be brought down before dusk, mother warned. "If night falls on your laundry you will have to rewash it," she said to Um Fadel, who bellowed back, *Aynaya ya sitt*, meaning, I'd give you my eyes if you asked, to which mother responded, *Tislam aynayki*, may your eyes be spared. This exchange of courtesies, compliments, and banter was part of a day's work and part of our culture too. Mother fed the washerwoman lunch and let her rest in the early afternoon, and they drank strong, sweet tea before going up to collect the dry laundry. Mother counted what was in the piles before folding to make sure nothing was missing. She paid Um Fadel by the day and gave her food to take home to her family or some clothing we no longer needed.

The laundry was sent out to be ironed the next day or the day after. In Egypt, ironing is a man's profession and the one who irons is called a *makwagi*. Ours was Abu Aryaan, a Copt whose shop was just around the corner. He picked up the shirts, pants, house dresses, anything that needed ironing; mother counted yet again, placed the laundry in a *bu'ga* (a large, square cloth), knotted the corners, and warned Abu Aryaan to be careful not to pop the buttons or singe the shirts. He always said, *haader, ya sitt, sama'an wa taa'ah*, meaning, he heard her and would comply. Each family's *bu'ga* was distinctive, some embroidered, others decorated with colorful patches, some plain. The laundry was returned neatly pressed, trousers on hangers, which mother returned to Abu Aryaan when she paid him. He charged 1 piaster per shirt and 2 per pair of trousers, less than a nickel.

Our household consisted of my parents, my two sisters, Sawsan and Salwa, and three brothers, Habib, Amin, and the baby, who came half a decade after me, Fikri. Our little servant girl was Samia. She had been hired from our family's village and her salary was paid directly to her father. This was common practice. I hated to see children used in this way and vowed thereafter never to have a servant. And I never have.

My father and mother were first cousins. It was the custom for cousins to marry and it is still not uncommon in Egypt today.

In fact, cousin marriages are expected. It was often said that the one you know is better than the one you don't know, and the fear of strangers was one of the reasons why cousin marriages were encouraged. The other reason was, of course, to keep property in the family, as so much agricultural land was owned in common by members of an entire family. Even trees such as date palms, which were a source of income, were owned by members of a family even if the land on which they grew was owned by another.

In some instances, if a young man refused to marry his cousin, it was considered a disgrace to his family. They accused him of lack of family feeling. "What's wrong with him? How can he refuse? What is he thinking? There's nothing wrong with her! She's not missing an arm or a leg, is she? She's not crippled, is she? She doesn't have pustules! She's as beautiful as a full moon! What can he object to?!" And so went the blame and laments. Such a refusal was a serious offense, an insult to the family whose daughter was rejected. If no solution was found, people could harbor resentment toward the guilty party and lifelong grudges too.

My father, however, loved my mother. So in their case it was a happy union from the start. He was older than she was and had watched her grow into a beautiful, intelligent young woman. In a sense, he had waited for her. He was thirty when they married. She was fifteen.

After graduating from primary school, my father helped his father with the management of their land in the village and saw a lot of his little cousin. But when he turned eighteen, he applied to the Ministry of Education for a job and got one. So he began teaching with only his primary school education, which was not uncommon at the time, as it was a solid education. When he was ready to marry, his salary was 6 Egyptian pounds a month, greater than the average 3 pounds a month paid many other teachers.

Father's family owned land in Ashmunayn. After his father died he inherited his portion of his father's land. The area around Ashmunayn was of interest to archeologists, as the ground was full of antiquities. Any time you dug, you dug up ancient Egyptian and Roman artifacts. Every time a farmer took a plow to the ground, he ran into a piece of history. Among the villagers, legend had it that buried treasure abounded and was guarded by a *rageeb*, a supernatural entity in the guise of an animal, male or female, a being with magical powers. One had to come to an agreement with this *rageeb* before taking anything from the ground. It was all fantasy, of course, but people believed such stories.

Before my parents married, father had traveled to Cairo to take a position teaching at a school in the Fagallah district. All his life, Daoud Bestawros was ambitious. As a young man, he looked beyond the Saeed for opportunities to improve himself. The capital seemed the place to go. Once hired, he arranged to live in Sakakini, a district of the city established by a Syrian Egyptian family, members of the Maronite aristocracy. Sakakini Pasha had acquired great wealth. During the building of the Suez Canal, workers digging the channel were plagued by rats. Many fell ill and even died after being bitten. The Pasha came up with an idea to combat the infestation. He hired people to gather street cats and paid a sum for each crateful of cats, which he then shipped to the construction sites. They were let loose to great effect and he prospered.

Sakakini Pasha used his wealth to build a palace, which is now a museum occupying a huge circle called Midan Sakakini. Daoud Bestawros described it in its glory days when the turrets and intricate masonry shone and the gardens were beautifully landscaped and maintained. The Sakakini palace was a sandstone and marble splendor; its lush circular garden was surrounded by wrought-iron fencing, painted black each year, and accessible through a massive iron gate that was always locked at night and guarded. Around the palace, he built apartment complexes that were rented out, and it is in one of these that my father lived with his uncle when he first moved to Cairo. As it was frowned on for a single man to live alone, my father lived with the family in their three-bedroom apartment on the third floor of one of these buildings. Their balcony overlooked the palace.

Father taught social studies. His students and their families looked up to him as they did to all teachers. Education being a privilege of the few, teachers were revered, their advice and counsel sought by family, parents, neighbors, everyone. They were known as the keepers of knowledge and respected as such. Generations of children depended on them and these children were considered the building blocks of the nation. Father was granted even more respect when he became a secondary school teacher, having received extra training by the time he married my mother, Demiana.

There were no more than thirty secondary schools in all of Egypt at the time my father started to teach in them. There was one in Cairo and one in each of the outlying provinces. Public schools were government run, but students still had to pay 20 Egyptian pounds a year as fees for books and supplies. Twenty pounds was a big chunk of money for most families and therefore only those who could afford to pay went. The fees were abolished only when the visionary Taha Hussein declared that education was a basic human right, that it should be free as air and water and available to all citizens. Despite being blind and coming from a poor, rural family, he achieved a high degree of education and was adviser to the Ministry of Education from 1950 to 1952.

My mother and father married in their village of Ashmunayn. The wedding was at home and lasted several hours, as was customary. Two priests officiated, offering the long wedding mass and traditional prayers. Mother must have been a beautiful bride. She was tall, fair, hazel eyed, and blessed with long, wavy, honey-colored hair. She also had a sweet disposition, which luckily for my father offset his impatient nature. He was quick to take offense and to react and had a quick temper. He was not unkind, but people were wary around him. People respected him, some feared him, some disliked him, but all loved my mother. Mother taught my siblings and me some important life lessons, notably, that it was of no use to hold a grudge. She demonstrated rather than taught charity. When beggars came to the door, she fed them, punishing any one of us children who thought it funny to tease them because of their clothes or their looks. I remember one of my brothers running circles around an old beggar, taunting him: "Old man, old man, your nose as big as a pitcher, catch me, catch me if you can." Amin was joined by Fikri, the youngest of my brothers, in taunting the old beggar, until mother chased them out. She gave the man a glass of tea and later said to all of us: "Never taunt someone less fortunate, and remember that misfortune is blind. You could wake up one morning and find that you are this beggar you made fun of." She also frequently reminded us to be humble and compassionate, saying, "Many are those ready to beat the camel when he's down," an old proverb and one of many she used to teach us. Her words, spoken when she was years younger than I am today, have remained with me. I try to honor her wisdom.

Prior to their wedding, my parents and their families, like all middle-class Egyptian families, prepared and furnished their home. Furniture, crockery, kitchenware, linens, everything needed to start housekeeping and likely to remain with the couple for the rest of their lives, was bought. The bride's family was responsible for providing the bedroom furniture, for example. The groom's family was likely to provide the living room set and even the dining room set. The most important room was the parlor where guests would be received, and hence it was the fanciest room in the house, the showpiece of the home. The groom's family was happy to boast that they had provided the furniture for it. If a family had modest means, the bedrooms and family room could be modest.

My father had his own ideas of what he wanted for his home, however, and had saved money for a dining-room suite of his own design. He ordered it from a cabinetmaker a full year before the wedding and paid for it in full when it was delivered within the year. He also bought a set of Austrian-made dishes that my brother Habib has now. It is missing a few pieces that broke over the years, but we all remember it well. It came with two double dishes for salt and pepper in the form of tiny baskets, which we children played with and probably broke. The complete set included a soup terrine, serving dishes, and two fruit stands. The cutlery service for twelve was Sheffield, the knives finished with bone handles. My sisters Sawsan and Salwa have a few pieces each, but most disappeared over time, lost or stolen. There was also a set of glasses with gold borders. All these were used only on special occasions or when my parents had company. The rest of the time we ate on everyday white dishes. One of the things my father insisted on, however, was the use of a white tablecloth at all times. There was a cloth for everyday use and another, a damask tablecloth with napkins, for special meals. Was this an expression of personal taste? Something he had observed in the homes of the missionaries? One thing was certain, my father admired British culture. He sought out and acquired books of English literature and owned a full set of Shakespeare that he read until the day he died. He also loved the Arabic classics and had a good collection as well as quantities of religious books and tracts, many given to him or purchased from the Protestant missionaries we called the Balamos, the Plymouth Brothers with whom he had associated himself when he converted.

My mother was a devout Copt and a traditional woman in every respect. Growing up, she had received some education at an American school in Assiut, but had no inclination to convert to Protestantism. She learned to read and write. The only book I saw her read, however, was the Holy Bible, which she read in Arabic. Although mother went with father to his Protestant prayer meetings, she never wavered from her Coptic faith. She quietly raised us children with a dedication to the Coptic Church and with pride in our heritage. She encouraged us to be steadfast, explaining that we were thus not only Christians but also patriots. Beneath her gentle demeanor she had a strong personality that she imparted to all of her children, particularly my oldest brother and me.

Father clung fast to the Balamos although he had been born and raised in the Coptic Church. Was his conviction born of some longing to be modern? Did he view the West as progressive and Protestant theology as liberating? Be this as it may, he was progressive in theory perhaps, but a traditional man through and through when it came to his family. Was his conversion part of a trend in his day? In Upper Egypt particularly, Protestants drew many young Copts away from our ancestral church. Whatever the reason, it was a source of friction between my parents and my mother considered it a sort of betrayal.

Father was deeply religious and he wished to impose his beliefs on his children. He preached to us with no respite and no explanation. His attempts at persuading my mother and his children to follow him into the Protestant faith failed. This was in part due to his inclination to do more talking than listening. My mother was patient with my father and followed his directions, but quietly let him know her thoughts. He respected her and appreciated her role in keeping balance and harmony in the family. She had a gift for listening and was loved by all for her wisdom and skill as a mediator. More than once I overheard her saying to my father, "Oh Daoud, this habit of yours will make people shrink away from you. You must be more patient." She was talking about his tendency to make repetitious demands of others and to be pedantic. This annoyed his wife, his children, his colleagues, and even the poor servant girl, who, of course, could not open her mouth to say a word anyway.

My father was educated, well read, ambitious, and intelligent. He might have done more with his life had he not been so inflexible. His impatience was his worst enemy. Each one of us children inherited personality traits from our parents. Some of these traits have served us well whereas others have not.

At home, father held prayer meetings daily. We had to attend, but because he was tedious, our minds wandered. Fikri thought of games he wanted to play, Sawsan of her embroidery, Salwa of her knitting, and I could hardly wait to get back to my latest mystery novel. When we reached the age of seven or so, father expected us to say prayers. I remember one Habib said. He must have been dreaming of the meal awaiting us and shouted, "Oh, Lord, let there be *mulukhiyya* for lunch today!" We all giggled, but a stern look from father instantly silenced us. Father took his prayer meetings seriously, but what could he say to Habib? What did a child of seven know of prayer or of how to pray? Mother, ever the dutiful observer, said nothing though I detected a smile.

We children understood little of father's lectures and sermons. What did this word "sin" that came up all the time mean? I thought it must be whatever made me feel guilty and for which I would be punished. I might only have been five or six when fear entered my life. Fear too was what I felt as a teenager when my parents recounted their experiences of the revolution of 1919, calling it the *hogah*, or uprising. Although it took place a decade before I was born, I never stopped wondering if we would again hear gunshots as they had and see people wounded and dying in the streets. This countrywide revolution was directed against the British occupation of Egypt and led to Britain's recognition of Egyptian independence in 1922, even though Britain refused to relinquish its hold on the Suez Canal, which happened only after the 1952 revolution.

But to get back to childhood memories of family life. My father read to us from a book called *The Golden Texts*. Again, we were bored because nothing was explained in a way a young mind could understand. We were educated in the same way at school, where learning was by rote memorization. When I was five, my parents sent me to a private school to learn the English language. My first teacher, Miss Qawkab, was a bitter, sadistic woman. She was tall, gaunt, and wore her graying hair in a thick braid twisted like a crown on top of her head. I thought of it as a crown full of thorns to prick us children with. Her eyes bulged and I feared her as if she were a monster. She hit our hands with the edge of a ruler, ordered us to kneel with our faces to the wall, and worst of all, made us stand holding a chair above our heads until we collapsed. This she did at the slightest provocation. One day, when I could no longer stand to be in Miss Qawkab's presence, I ran away. At recess, I hid behind the gatekeeper's post and bolted the moment he was distracted. I didn't know my way home, nor did I know anything about the streets around the school. I wandered until I got to a quiet street with a grassy knoll and shade trees in the middle. I sat under the trees and soon fell asleep. When I was discovered missing, word was sent to my father. He came and confronted Miss Qawkab, who apparently shrieked: "Where is the boy? Where is the boy? He was here moments ago. Can a boy melt like a lump of rock salt in water?!" I was her responsibility and she was no doubt afraid of the consequences of my disappearance. The school, grounds, neighborhood, every nook and cranny was searched. The search produced no Nader, and when I grew up and remembered the day I thought I had indeed lived up to my name since Nader means rare. When the police found me asleep in my little grassy refuge an officer tapped me on the shoulder and I woke up startled and afraid. He said, "Don't be afraid, I'm taking you home." When I saw my mother I cried. She comforted me, and my father for once was patient. He asked why I had run away and I told him that Miss Qawkab terrified me. Surprisingly, he understood, and transferred me to another school where instruction was in Arabic.

The new school was only a slight improvement. This time, the teacher was a Muslim cleric, Sheikh Abd al Siddik. He was a tall, lazy, mean man. He spent his time chatting with his colleagues and sipping tea and he loved to frighten us. To do this he had developed a little routine: He gave us an assignment and declared, "I want absolute silence." He then stepped out of the classroom and returned suddenly to surprise us and shout, "Who was talking? I heard talking, there was talking, who was talking?! The pupil who was talking will stand up!" He then waved his arms around and finally pointed randomly at a child. "You! Yes, you! Stand up! You were talking, I heard you, I saw you!" The kid got a thrashing and the sheikh went back out. He repeated these incursions at least twice a day until the room was silent as a tomb and felt like one too.

Somehow I weathered that year without a beating and was then ready for first grade and public school. It was my first experience really at formal education. Unlike the private schools, which were a catchall for problem kids, most often rich kids, the public schools had a rigorous curriculum set and supervised by the Ministry of Education, which maintained very high standards at the time. You could not buy your way into them. Today, they are lacking in good instruction and most parents are bamboozled into hiring the classroom teachers to give their children costly private lessons in order to insure their safe passage from one grade to another. These practices blend in with other forms of corruption rampant in present-day Egypt.

But let me tell you about my first year of school. The first year of public school went well for me. I was studious and eager, the teachers were capable, and my fellow students and I were excited to be learning. That year I turned eight. When the year was over, father told us we would henceforth be spending summers in our village. This meant that we left Assiut in May and returned in October. He also told us that, after we returned to school, he would travel to Ashmunayn periodically to manage his agricultural land in an effort to improve yields. So on a very hot day in May, everything was at the ready, and the day after school let out, we departed by train. When we arrived, our relatives awaited us with three cars to convey us and our luggage to our family home. One car was for mother, the girls and the youngest of us, and the servant girl. The second car was for father, the oldest boys, and the luggage. The third car was to carry back the relatives who had come to meet our train.

In 1927, my grandfather died and left my father 5 acres of rich agricultural property that, by his efforts and good management, he increased to 30 before his death. Father decided he could improve his estate by being present as often as possible, overseeing the planting, fertilizing, and harvesting of the crops. He rented the land to peasants who farmed it and he took a share of the profits in addition to the rents. He grew cotton, wheat, corn, and sugarcane. When it was time to harvest any of his crops, father made sure he was in the village. He either sold the crops or stored them to sell later at a better market price. This is how he left us something we could start our own lives with, a sort of leavening for each of his children to build on, a nest egg.

Our life in the village was a collective life. The extended family lived under one roof, eating together and functioning as a unit. The house had three distinct wings. Our family had one wing and my mother's brothers had the other two. Of course they were first cousins and there was shared property.

The house itself was built in the nineteenth century and modernized with an indoor bathroom added in 1915, just prior to my maternal grandfather's wedding. The kitchen and other shared spaces such as the utility rooms on the roof and the courtyard were original to the house. So were the high-ceilinged living room and dining room, which had composite marble tile floors. The living room was furnished with a heavy dark-wood sofa and four chairs covered in wine-red velvet trimmed with heavy gold fringes that I liked to play with as a toddler, and there was a matching table in between. The dining-room table was walnut with matching chairs and a glass-fronted glassware cabinet that my mother cherished. She made lace doilies for the shelves. In one corner was a blue enameled cast-iron stove to warm the room on winter nights. It was coal fueled. As to the sleeping rooms, the arrangement was simple. Boys were in one room and girls in another and each set of parents had their private bedroom. The bedroom floors were wood.

Our country cousins looked forward to our arrival, as we brought gifts of candy for the kids, cloth for uncles and aunts to fashion dresses and kaftans, scarves, and shawls, and delicacies from the city. They rarely left Ashmunayn other than to visit relatives in nearby villages, and so our presence every summer gave them a sense of renewal. The Christians, in our rural areas in particular, intermarried and remained a close-knit group. Relatives came to visit soon after we arrived and we reciprocated, riding donkeys or camels to get to other villages, or driving by automobile.

At harvest time, we all went to the fields. We were observers, not workers, unlike peasant children our age who were already doing backbreaking work. At the time of cotton harvest they carried double sacks of cotton, one long pouch in front, one slung on their backs, which were weighed by the overseer who paid them at the end of each day. Each sack was put on the scales and the name of the harvester registered in a mammoth ledger. This overseer sat at an old wooden table placed in the shade of a white mulberry tree, calling out, "Boy so and so, or girl so and so, come forward. You have harvested this many pounds, or that many pounds, here are your wages." Their earnings went directly to the parents.

For wheat harvest, the *norag* was used and we liked to ride on its wide seat as it went round and round, its steel wheels thrashing and separating chaff from grain. Corn was husked and dried, and men stood in a circle with sticks and thrashed it to remove the kernels from their cobs. It was grueling work in the hot sun, and by the time their wives brought them lunch in the fields and they ate under the mulberry tree, their hands were raw from thrashing. They were paid 30 piasters a day, about 50 cents. You could still feed a family on such wages, especially in the countryside.

It was customary for children to socialize with their peers and generally we did not play with older or younger siblings or cousins. A five-year difference between playmates was the norm. It was believed that peers understood each other's games and conversation and were thus best suited to be buddies and companions.

One summer, one of my peers sounded an alarm that saved my life. There was a huge room in the house called the grain room. It was used for wheat storage. An opening in the ceiling allowed grain to be funneled in after harvest. The windows of this room were boarded up to hold in the grain and it served as a sort of silo. My cousin and I watched the transfer of grain and we were horsing around, playing as we watched. Suddenly I lost my balance and fell into the opening along with the grain. I could have suffocated if my cousin had not shouted for help, bringing the adults in a hurry. As if by some miracle, the pressure of the grain on the windows blew out one of the windows and the grain rushed out, taking me along with it, where the adults caught me and I was saved.

Things happen to children. Sometimes unseen forces intervene. The family chalked up my survival to a miracle and went to church to pray, lighting candles and offering thanks. The grain was restored, the window boarded up, and a stern warning delivered to me. I never played there again.

Death tried catching up with me a few years later and again I survived. I came down with typhoid fever at a time when there were no drug cures available. I was put to bed for forty days in a darkened room. Father forbade my siblings from coming near me for fear of infection, and my mother sat vigil at my side, day and night. She wept and prayed, dozed and woke, applied vinegar compresses to my body and never left me. Late one night, in the second week of my illness, she felt a hand on her shoulder. She sat up with a start and saw a diaphanous figure retreating into the darkness. She was convinced it was the Virgin Mary who had come and performed another miracle, as the next day my fever broke.

I have brushed shoulders with death since a boy, as you can see, and when I turned ten, I saw typhoid carry off my mother's youngest sister, Sattoota. She left behind six children, the eldest, Maurice, sixteen years old. Uncle Sayfayn, her husband, wept and wailed in his grief. "To whom have you left me and your orphans, Sattoota? To whom have you left me?!" Some said that he behaved like a woman, but you must understand that the union of aunt Sattoota and uncle Sayfayn was the biggest love story of the family, not just an arranged marriage between cousins. He was inconsolable. He was a wealthy man and owned a lot of land that was said to be some of the most fertile in the region. He was also blessed with a silver tongue and the gift to make money on any venture he undertook. He bought low and sold high, is what people said, and his timing, self-confidence, and steadfast faith in God were his greatest attributes. He was kind and generous too. Like my father he was a member of the Anglican Church, of which the Plymouth Brethren was a conservative branch, going back to nineteenth-century Ireland. My uncle had joined their prayer meetings as a young man and raised his children as Protestants, giving them all European names. His sons were Maurice, Gabriel, Emmanuel, and Samuel, and his daughters, Mary and Elizabeth. When aunt Satoota died, Maurice left school and devoted himself to running the household, educating and caring for his younger siblings and helping his father. He had inherited his father's business sense and continued to care for his younger siblings after their father passed away just a year after his beloved Satoota.

In Egypt, and particularly in the Egyptian countryside, there is not a family without some sort of internal strife. Some discord eventually heals, but some enmities last a lifetime, occasionally carrying over from one generation to the next. Most often, quarrels revolve around property, water rights, inheritance, and personal and business alliances. Some are so serious that they lead to feuds and murders. The police never interfere because these are family matters and therefore must be left to families to deal with.

When Egyptian agricultural land was parceled into small-holdings donated by the *khedive* (viceroy of Egypt under Turkish rule, 1867–1914) people started to create boundaries, and so the troubles began. Vast tracts of land had initially been owned by Muhammad Ali, an Albanian commander of the Ottoman Army who was sent to drive Napoleon's forces from Egypt. When the French withdrew, he seized power and forced the Ottoman sultan, Mahmud the Second, to recognize him as *wali* (governor) of Egypt, and in 1805 seized all 600,000 or so acres of land for himself. Subsequently, he called himself *khedive* (viceroy), and has come down in history as the founder of modern Egypt. That's a long story and this is not the place for it.

Suffice it to say that when Egyptian agricultural land was under his control, it had been easy to determine boundaries and to administer effectively, even if the profits from these lands, especially from cotton crops, went directly into his pockets. But once the land was parceled out a few *kirats* here, a few *kirats* there (the *kirat* being a twenty-fourth part of a *feddan*, which is just a little over an acre), everything became more complicated. A parent might wonder, "When I die, how will my acre or two suffice to feed ten children?" Division of property was, and still is, at the heart of family conflicts.

Perennial irrigation was introduced to our village in 1935. I don't remember much about this or about the Nile rising except that, as a boy, I almost drowned in the river at the time of the floods. My father rented 40 *feddans* of land in a region about 5 miles from Ashmunayn. The land was directly on the Nile, a good place to grow sugarcane. He also built a small factory to make molasses. We went there with him when he supervised, especially as we liked to play with the peasant children who taught us to jump from the banks of the Nile into the river. The only problem was that I did not swim and when I tried it the current carried me away. Had it not been for one of the peasants jumping in after me, I would have surely drowned. Another brush with death was in the course of a ferryboat crossing. The boat sank. How did I survive? I honestly don't know. It could be that terror erased the memory.

Our family got together for religious feasts, weddings, and to celebrate the success of one of us passing exams. When we made high marks, we were rewarded with food and money. Mother made a favorite meal, served an extra piece of chicken to the successful pupil and father gave him or her 5 piasters in recognition, the equivalent of a few pennies. We were thrilled, as it meant we could get an extra book or extra supplies to add to what the school provided. A book was my greatest treat, as I loved to read and still do.

In primary and middle school, we used pens with nibs, which we dipped in ink. Fountain pens were allowed only in high school. We kept pen, pencils, pencil sharpener, and an eraser in a wood box, which we picked out from a stationer's shop at the start of primary school. It was an essential item in our school satchels and we usually kept it until we graduated.

Each classroom desk had a round opening on the top right-hand side. Into this hole was sunk a white porcelain inkwell. It was the school janitor's job to keep these filled with the purple ink used in schools. Throughout grade school, there was not a boy or girl whose hands or uniform was free from purple splotches!

As a child I had long hair. I was proud of it. One day, without warning, my father decided it was time to have it cut and made arrangements with the town barber. I was six, I think. Father called our little servant Samia and said to her, "Take this boy to *Usta* 'Ali and tell him to follow the instructions I left with him yesterday." Samia, who must have been twelve or thirteen at the time, did as she was told. She took me by the hand and walked me to the barbershop. I had no idea what instructions my father had left with *Usta* 'Ali but was shocked when I saw the locks of my curly hair falling all around me on the floor. The barber then shaved my head, and when I encountered my face in the mirror I wept bitterly.

I mourned my hair for days, refused to eat or listen to my mother's entreaties or words of comfort. All I could do was touch my head periodically in utter disbelief and cry. As soon as I had a say in what happened or did not happen to me, I let my hair grow and have worn it long ever since.

Childhood is full of storms. I remember being terrified of the *khamsin* winds in March and April. When the winds rose up and blew red dust and sand into every crevice of our home, my father gathered us around him to pray. Windows rattled and shutters clattered and the wind swept the streets, carrying paper and detritus through the city. If an incautious housewife happened to leave laundry on the line, it was gone too. I hung onto mother and my sisters and found my father's invocations almost as frightening as the winds.

The year of my shocking haircut, I learned that not all people are treated equally or justly, nor are children exempt from injustice or prejudice. I came to this realization when a boy at school hit me and the teacher favored him because he was from a prominent family, even though he had been the aggressor, not I. Later, when my family moved to the town of Helwan, where I met a relative of the founder of the Muslim Brotherhood and we became friends, I noticed that children of the rich were given special consideration. Muslim classmates were favored over Christians, as they were in the majority. I learned how to fend for myself that year, how to be guarded and avoid confrontation as much as possible, but it hurt me to feel my freedoms curtailed. This was the reality I was awakening to the year I turned ten.

But to return briefly to my childhood in Assiut. When I was old enough to go out with my siblings, a favorite outing of mine was the beautiful public park near our apartment building. On Fridays, a band played there in a white gazebo and people sat on the grass and listened. They played borrowed music like marches and I begged to go there to listen. Once in a while Samia and my sisters packed us into a horse-drawn carriage, a *hantur*, and off we went with this little girl who was not much older than some of us younger children, trying to keep us under control. In the carriage with its top down, two of us boys perched high beside the driver, the rest on the banquette in the coach. The smallest were ordered to the jump seats by my older sisters, who felt entitled to boss around both the younger kids and the little servant girl. Nobody liked it, but they were in charge and if we wanted to go to the park we had to mind them.

One year, father announced that he had been promoted at work but that the promotion required us to move to Qena. My mother was pleased with the promotion but not so pleased with the move to a town that had the reputation of being a hardship post because of its inclement climate and unfriendly inhabitants. It was settled between my parents, however, and my father went ahead of us to arrange for housing. We knew that he would look for something near the train station to facilitate his comings and goings to the village and that it had to be a top-floor apartment. We would be ready to leave in May, shortly after the end of the school year. We packed our furniture and belongings, which were sent to the train station on two donkey carts to be shipped to Qena as freight, and on the appointed day we boarded the passenger train for what seemed to be an interminable journey, as the train stopped in every village and town that had a train station. By the time we got to Qena, we were covered in dust, our hands and faces blackened by the soot blowing in the windows from the coal-fired locomotive, and we were tired and hot. Taxis took us to our new home on Shari'al Mahatta, Station Street, where our belongings had arrived ahead of us. We camped amidst our furniture and beds in a state of temporary disarray while one of my father's colleagues, a Muslim cleric who lived with his family in the apartment below ours, welcomed us and sent up a dinner to sustain us. We became friends and our association with this family was a positive experience in this unpleasant province. Qena was famous for its hot-tempered people and for nonstop feuding among families. We experienced our first shooting shortly after I started school. The school closed and parents were notified to come get their children. The reason for this was to prevent feuding families from harming each other's children. I will never forget this day because, through some oversight, my

father was not notified in time and I ended up anxiously waiting with no parent to rescue me. My neighbor, a boy my age,
was likewise stranded, so we kept each other company but also
stirred each other into a frenzy of fear. It seems that our fathers
were notified only long after the school closed, and when they
came they found two frightened little boys huddled together.

At school, I began to study Arabic literature and loved it.
I memorized excerpts from the *jahiliyya* (pre-Islamic) poets,
verses from the Qur'an, and stories like *Kalila wa Dimna*. I
couldn't get enough. We were called up before the class to recite
and I came to enjoy doing this. I also relished parsing, analyz-
ing, and explaining the grammatical value of lines from stories and poems. Our teacher tested us by picking a line from
an assigned text or from the middle of a poem and asking us to
complete it. Although I am a Christian and the Bible is my book,
I attended classes where we memorized and studied parts of the
Qur'an. The language is beautiful and the recitation melodious.
I remember Muslim classmates coming to school all puffed up
with pride at being able to recite long passages without error.
The spirit of competition was ignited in me then and I decided I
could best them. I set to committing Qur'anic as well as biblical
verses to memory. I proudly recited the first in school and the
second at home.

Our life outside of school was ordinary. There was little to
distinguish us from other middle-class Egyptian families of the
time. Boys and girls went to different schools and even at home
we were quasi-segregated. Sawsan and Salwa studied in one room
while Habib, Amin, Fikri and I were in another. My father had
had a local carpenter make identical desks for each of us with a
top that we could push open and that had a slight incline. The
top was also fitted with a hasp and a tiny padlock. My padlock
broke soon after I got the desk and just hung there looking either
useless or decorative, I'm not sure. We stored books, notebooks,

slates, chalk, pens and nibs, broad tip for Arabic script, narrow for Latin script, bottles of ink, pencils, erasers, pencil sharpeners, and odds and ends. We each received a set of colored pencils at the start of every year and these we enjoyed when making maps and drawing.

Our lives were routine. As soon as we got home from school and put away our things, we changed into a *galabeyya*, or lightweight kaftan. Father made it clear to us that we were never to go out in them, like "common folk," but should dress in slacks and a clean shirt with a pullover or jacket on top in winter for the boys. The girls wore dresses. Today, girls can wear slacks, but not then. It was the reverse when we were in the village and instructed to wear our *galabeyyas* in order to blend in. Our *galabeyyas*, just like our school clothes, were marked with purple blotches, the color of the ink we used at home and at school. Hard as the washerwoman tried, she could never completely take out these ink stains.

Every other year, father and mother outfitted each of their children with clothes as we grew and as needed. Clothes were also handed down. In preparation for school, father brought home bolts of shirting material for the boys and colorful cottons, which my mother picked out with him, for the girls. They also bought wool to make slacks and jackets as well as light woolens dresses for the girls. In addition, they purchased bolts of cotton flannel, striped for boys and flowered for girls, for winter nightwear.

When we began to spend the summers in the village, father brought us home at the beginning of October, two weeks before the start of school, so that mother could get us outfitted and ready for the year. To that end a seamstress was hired, a woman who had come recommended for her skill and honesty through someone at the church. Her name was Ferdous, but we called her auntie Doosa. She lived with us for ten days until the task was complete. Over the years she became one of the family, and the moment she arrived, my mother served her the thimbleful of bitter coffee loaded with sugar that she loved. Only then did the work begin with mother first explaining what we wanted done. Mother determined the cut of a boy's shirt, what kind of collar was required, what color dress suited each girl, what buttons to use on what, what frills or rickrack should trim a dress, what neckline would be best for a nightgown, and so on. She was sensitive to our likes and dislikes and made sure to consult us when it came to our clothing. She had an excellent Singer sewing machine that she herself used for smaller jobs. During these October marathons, she helped with the finishing work while the seamstress did the cutting and bulk of the sewing. They worked from dawn until dusk, the house buzzing with activity, comings and goings, the sound of the Singer's foot pedal, spoons stirring sugar in tea glasses, clatter of plates at meal times, chatter and laughter, and, in the midst of it all, my father's daily prayer meeting that even the seamstress had to attend. At the close of this frenzied two weeks, we wore our new clothes with pride and pleasure. Of course, the younger kids got the short end of the stick since they were handed down what the older ones had outgrown. But mother consoled them, saying that soon their turn would come for something new and that maybe she would have a special dress or a sweater ready for them for Christmas.

Whereas mother labored at home, father was responsible for everything we needed from the world outside the home. He took us to uncle Halim, the cobbler, to be measured for shoes and boots and to uncle Zaki, the tailor, for slacks and jacket.

I remember the high-topped shoes we wore that had buttons up one side to be hooked and unhooked with a buttonhook that we often lost. Fights broke out when one of us lost his hook and tried to borrow a brother's, and more often than not the boots were ill fitting and pinched. The unhappy child whose toes were pinched from the start limped for a few weeks. When the leather did not "ease" as uncle Halim claimed it would, father took the victim back to the cobbler to have a new pair made. Of course he reprimanded uncle Halim, saying, "Is this the best you can do for us, 'Am Halim? And here we have been your faithful clients all of these years! Can you sleep with a clear conscience when this poor child's foot is being injured in this way? Do you want him limping for the rest of his life?" Uncle Halim then protested, pointing out that it took time for the leather to stretch, that the foot had to mold to the shoe and a hundred other excuses. Finally, when there was nothing for it but to accommodate or lose his client, he agreed to make the poor boy a new pair. And so it went with uncle Halim and father drinking a cup of coffee together while all of this negotiating was going on.

Next came uncle Zaki, the tailor who specialized in slacks. My father took us to him to be measured and entrusted the tweed or wool into his hands, saying, "You will make slacks from this bolt for this boy, and slacks from that one for this one, and make sure this one has pleats in front and that one cuffs." Uncle Zaki listened patiently, ordered tea, and agreed to everything. He made anywhere from six to ten pairs of pants at one time and, as there were two years between each of us boys, pants were handed down, serving two boys before wearing out. We wore slacks and shirts with open collars in summer and suits in winter.

Our lives were organized around work, school, family, meals, rest and relaxation, and church. There was no social life to speak of, at least not in the sense that we understand it today. I believe that socializing as we do today is quite a modern concept. We had no such thing as parties, although people attended weddings and funerals, baptisms, or exchanged visits with ritualized reciprocity, and conventions were understood by all and strictly observed. Friends were divided into two groups: close friends and acquaintances. With close friends, the husband and wife came to visit together. With acquaintances, only the men came. When a couple came calling, the husband sat with father in the drawing room while the wife sat with mother in the family room. Visits exchanged between women were another form of relationship and father had nothing to do with these. The men who visited father alone were generally colleagues from school, business associates, or folks from Ashmunayn attending to matters regarding the land.

Church members also called on us, both men and women. Visiting between couples was usually agreed on ahead of time. People would say, "We are coming to have a cup of coffee with you tomorrow," for example. Father's response was the standard, *Ahlan wa sahlan*, you are most welcome. No food was served and only family came to meals. Guests were offered tea or coffee and at feast times mother served *kahk*, tiny hard cakes filled with a rich honey and butter or date and butter mixture and dusted with powdered sugar. These cakes were served only at feast times.

Conversation too was formal, conducted around acceptable topics and interspersed with ritual phrases, expressions, proverbs, and compliments. Everyone understood and used certain forms of social courtesies. A guest might say, "We are happy to see you," to which the host could respond, "You have filled our home with light." The guest might best him with an even greater compliment such as, "Your light is quite sufficient and illuminates our city," and so on. It was not unusual for this to be the meat of the visit, and these exchanges were, and still are, called *mugamala*.

There were also topics of conversation that were gender specific. Men focused on politics, prices of goods and services, land, crops, education, the weather. Women, on the other hand, gossiped and talked about children and household problems. They discussed the boys and the girls, the problems of the boys and the girls, the chaos created by the boys and the girls, the untidy habits of the boys and the girls, the lack of cleaning implements and help, the difficulty of keeping house, and so on. Nothing was ever said of a truly personal nature, however, and family affairs were well-guarded secrets.

During the school year, our days started with breakfast, served by mother around 7 o'clock. We had tea with milk, bread-sticks, feta cheese, and hard-boiled eggs. Every few days we had Egypt's national dish, *ful medammes*, fava beans. Mother picked over the beans and cleaned them, taking out small pebbles, sticks, mud. She soaked the beans and simmered them all night long in a special pot with narrow neck. At breakfast she dressed them with oil, lemon, salt, pepper, and cumin and served them with chopped tomato and green onions. Bread, of course, was our *baladi* bread, which is a form of pita, but denser, darker, and chewier, the bottom crusted with bran. Mother also made fresh angel-hair noodles certain mornings, a dish we all loved. She cooked and served them with warm milk and sugar. She also made *basees*, a rich cereal consisting of cracked wheat and flour slowly cooked in milk and served with clarified butter and sugar.

Our diet was healthy and we always ate at home. Breakfast fortified us for the day and lunch was the big meal, which we ate around 2 o'clock in the afternoon. We had rice, soups, stews cooked with or without meat, and chicken, boiled then fried in butter and sprinkled with salt, pepper, and *buhar*, allspice. We also had vegetables stuffed with rice and ground meat, or with rice and green herbs when we fasted. There are many fasts observed by Copts. One of my favorites is during the month of August, when mother made cabbage rolls with rice and dill, grape leaves with rice, onion, and mint, green peppers with rice, garlic, and parsley, and tomatoes with rice, onions, and all-spice. She always served a salad of romaine lettuce, tomatoes, and cucumbers dressed with lime juice and cumin. Sometimes we had *gargeer*, arugula. I believe that Egyptian fruits have no equals, and they were plentiful and eaten always in season. We had bananas, oranges, tangerines, dates, mangoes, guavas, pears, and sometimes apples. Mother made rice or other puddings perfumed with rose or orange-blossom water and also *balooza*, a gelatinous dessert, nicknamed "fatso" because it wiggled when carried to the table, causing much giggling among the children.

Like most middle-class women, mother never went out alone. If she had an errand or was going to church, one of us or the new little servant girl, Maryam, went along. She never went to the market. In fact, it was considered demeaning for her to do so and would have shamed her if she had had to. Father stocked her pantry very well with bulk goods and she stored these items in a room called the *karaar*. Some of these items, such as flour in 100-pound sacks, cheese in tall, straight-sided tins, and butter in round, sealed tins, were ordered months in advance and arrived by train from the village and to the house by a horse- or donkey-drawn cart.

Father did all of the shopping and sometimes took one of us boys or little Maryam to help carry things home. Maryam was never allowed to go out alone, however, nor was she ever trusted with more than a few pennies if it was necessary for her to go around the corner on some quick errand. It was feared that she could be snatched or might run away. I hated how she was treated, how working children were treated, how servants were suspected always of thievery and deceit, never trusted. Servants, peasants, apprentices, their lot was often harsh. They were overworked, underpaid, subjected to verbal and physical abuse, their lives often tragic. A servant girl earned about 15 piasters a month (less than 25 cents), paid to her family. She was clothed and fed by the family she worked for, often fed leftovers, and referred to as a "plate licker" because she was so hungry she was purported to lick anything left over on the plates. Humiliating! She rarely had a room of her own, often sleeping on a pallet on the kitchen floor. Many families were kind, but most were not, and servants were really little more than slaves.

One time, before we left Qena, I took it into my head to become a vegetarian. I read and greatly admired the tenth-century ascetic poet Abu Ala' al Me'arry, who never touched meat. I wanted to be like him and so declared to my family that I never wanted to kill and never wanted to eat an animal ever again. I wrote down my intentions on a scrap of paper, hid the paper under a carpet, and this was to serve as my vow and reminder if my resolve weakened.

One day I said to my mother, "Imagine if animals cut off our necks, sliced our flesh, and fried it for eating, what would we think? I will never again touch meat!" Mother said, "If this is the case, Nader, my son, what would you like me to cook for you?" I said, "I will cook for myself." She asked, "And what will you cook?" I said, "Boiled vegetables." She persisted, "Why do you want to do this? Why not just eat with your brothers and sisters like a proper human being?" I dug in my heels and so she declared, "Stupid boy, do you want to kill yourself?" I made some self-righteous remark, then asked, "Can I use the stove?" She bided her time, I know now, until I came to my senses. She simply said, "You'll have to wait until I've cooked for the family first."

I waited, thinking of my poet and feeling superior. When mother finished, I got a pan, put salt and water in it, tossed in the vegetables, but was distracted away from the hissing Primus stove. When I remembered my meal on the stove and ran back to get it, the water had evaporated and my vegetables were scorched. This was the beginning and end of my vegetarianism. I retrieved the vow from under the rug, threw it in the trash, and turned to my mother, who simply put a plate of food on the table before me without comment. This was the end of my vegetarian experiment though I continued to love the poet who inspired it and still do.

I did not have an adolescence in the true sense of that word. I was aware of changes in my body and I felt my emotions roiling while a sort of electric charge set me apart from the boy I remembered myself to be. I never spoke to my parents about what I was feeling. It was just not done. I weathered and escaped into literature and my imagination. It was not until we moved to the town of Helwan when I turned fifteen that I had a chance to interact with girls who were not family members. We just talked. Nothing more was permitted or acceptable. Of course a boy my age in rural Egypt might already have entered into marriage and been initiated to sexual matters, but not so us city boys.

We moved to Helwan when my father got another promotion. We were excited and glad to leave Qena. Helwan, a town on the Nile south of Cairo, had a salubrious climate, mineral springs, clean air, and good water. It was a healthy place to live and father found us a top-floor apartment with a huge balcony from which we could glimpse the Nile and watch *fellucas*, sail boats, and *ayyasas*, wooden cargo sailboats, going up and down the river. Because only their sails were visible above the buildings between us and the river, they looked like passing phantoms. When we strolled along the Nile, which we did almost daily, we saw them close up under full sail, artfully loaded with cargos of pottery packed in straw to protect them from breakage, or bricks, hay bales, or rocks. They were used for heavy transport. If a boat coming passed a boat going in the other direction, one boatman shouted to the other, *Itfaddal, shai*, come have tea. Of course, neither could stop and the invitation was at best a courtesy. The saying, *'Uzumit marakbeyya*, a boatman's invitation, came to mean an offer made in word only.

Down below our balcony, in a huge house across the street, lived a rich merchant called 'Am Ghaleb. He had four wives and every time he divorced one of them the whole neighborhood knew about it because of their yelling and fighting. My sister Sawsan reflected that the rich had nothing better to do.

'Am Ghaleb spent most of his time outdoors in his garden. He ate, slept, and sat on a bench in plain view of the neighborhood and quarreled incessantly with his wives. This was his life and he became the butt of jokes on our street. I heard a lot about 'Am Ghaleb and his affairs from my sisters and my mother, who gossiped with other women, making veiled remarks about him and his wives.

Divorce was easy among Muslims, but almost impossible among Christians. If ever a Christian did manage to divorce, tongues wagged and you could hear the women say, "He's caught the disease from 'Am Ghaleb."

Helwan was different from all the towns we had lived in. It was clean and beautiful and the air was healthy. It had natural springs and was a wintering destination for the rich, even the king. Egypt's first sanatorium for the treatment of lung disease, under the direction of Dr. Abd al Raouf Hassan, was well known not only in Egypt but also internationally. Dr. Hassan was a great man.

Helwan had a large middle-class population living typical middle-class lives. They had comfortable apartments for 3 or 4 pounds a month rent, and the rents are controlled to this day. Landlords then found themselves in a bind, not being able to meet the rising costs of maintaining their properties. These beautiful buildings have decayed over time, becoming eyesores. When we lived in Helwan, however, our apartment was in a relatively new and well-maintained three-story limestone building, typical of such buildings constructed in the 1920s, 30s and 40s. It had seven large rooms, a large kitchen, and two large balconies. On the floor below us lived a Polish family of the Hebrew faith. The father was mean, especially to one of his sons. Every now and again we heard yelling and crying and someone said, "Alexi's getting a beating!" We ran out on the balcony to see. This was the first Jewish family I had ever encountered. The mother was kind and came to the boy's rescue and we saw her consoling him. I never understood why the father was so mean.

In my last year of primary school, around the time of the Second World War, one of my teachers was a Muslim fundamentalist who soon left teaching to take an important post in the Ministry of Education in Cairo. This same man was subsequently accused of plotting to overthrow the government and was condemned to death by Gamal Abdel Nasser. His nephew had been one of my classmates and we remained friends through college. We were a lot alike temperamentally and physically. We were both of us quiet, retiring, small at the time, and younger than most of our classmates. I appreciated his intelligence and the fact that we could discuss literature, philosophy, and current affairs.

Often in those years in Helwan there were student strikes. He and I participated only under duress, and despite the fact that I was a Copt and he a Muslim, he invited me to his home and I met his family, who were very decent people and made me feel welcome.

Years later, after we had each of us gone our separate ways—I was posted to Qena and he to a nearby town where he served as a district attorney—we met again and reminisced. I even stayed with him for a couple of nights during one of our visits and we talked about our college days and our fantasy sweethearts. There were no real sweethearts, of course, since in those days even exchanging more than a glance or a word with a girl was unthinkable.

But I'm getting ahead of myself. For me, those Helwan years were formative years. I was in high school and beginning to be aware of social and political issues. Some of my classmates were boys from powerful political families who came to school bellowing and bragging about the student strikes they were going to lead. They insisted everyone participate. Really, they left us no choice. The strike organizer was chosen not only because of his family connections but also his size: he was the tallest and strongest of the boys. He stood at the school gate and ordered a lockdown. "Don't set one foot beyond this gate," he ordered. Or, "Stand over here! Do this or do that!" Of course on some level we welcomed the excitement. We stood, marched, made a lot of noise, and echoed our leader, shouting, "Down with so and so," most often the British.

In Helwan, there was a large hospital for the Allied forces, some four hundred rooms. It had once been Khedive Abbas's palace, then one of the royal family's many residences until they turned it over to the British. It went from being an elegant hotel for people coming to soak in the beneficial mineral waters of Helwan, to take the cure, to an abandoned structure that eventually came under the aegis of the British because of an agreement Britain made with Egypt. This agreement stipulated that in case of war, Egyptian soil and property would serve the British crown. This was one of the things the students were protesting.

I tried to stay clear of these protests when I saw the police arrive and begin to beat people. They arrested the organizers, but with a telephone call from a prominent family member of one or more of these boys, they were set free at once. Most were from well-known families that the authorities did not dare to cross. One year, there were so many demonstrations that we attended school for only five months.

Social standing played such a big part in our lives that when two boys from one of the leading families beat up the principal of our school, the poor man could do nothing about it. He was of a lower class. He was small, chubby, red faced, and stood helpless in his wrecked office, furniture broken around him, torn papers littering the floor. The boys got a slap on the wrist.

We left Helwan before the war was over. Father worried about the air raids and declared one day that it was no longer safe to stay where we were. He had requested and been granted a transfer, and he was moving us back to Upper Egypt, to Assiut. Since the railroads were at the disposal of the British Army at the time, we could not move our belongings by train. So father hired space on board an *ayyasa* sailing south and all of our belongings went with it.

On the day of our move, the boat was moored at an appointed spot. Our furniture and belongings as well as father's collection of some three hundred books, packed in burlap bags, were taken there on three donkey carts. The boatmen, who were oafs, dumped everything higgledy-piggledy into the hold. The books were first, followed by the furniture, baskets of crockery and kitchen utensils, and other household items as well as suitcases on top. The boat sailed and before long the hull sprang a leak. By the time it arrived in Assiut the books were a soggy mess. We salvaged what we could by placing volumes on the roof to dry in the hot sun, and recovered some one hundred. The rest had to be thrown away. My father's library was sadly diminished.

I must tell you that something special happened to me during this book-rescue operation, however. As I sorted, cleaned, and dried them they took on a life of their own and came to mean far more to me than printed pages held between bindings. They energized me and I realized and understood in a flash that books were repositories of a strength I needed to nourish, educate, and entertain me. This was when my lifelong love of books really took root.

Soon after our return to Assiut, I joined the municipal library in town and began to devour novel after novel, many in translation. I read seventeen volumes of *Rocamboule* in a pocket edition. These were translated from the French by Mr. Tanios Abdo, an Egyptian of Syrian descent. I dove into *The Count of*

Monte Cristo, the adventures of Arsene Lupin—pronounced "Arseen Lubeen" by Arabic speakers who interchange *b*s and *p*s. I loved *The Adventures of Sherlock Holmes* and countless other books, mysteries, and thrillers.

Mr. Shafik Asad Farid, an Egyptian civil servant and a Copt, translated all of Sherlock Holmes while sitting at Groppi, the upscale Swiss-owned café on Kasr el Nil Street in Cairo. I met him years later and he explained to me that he had seven siblings at home and no place to work. "I knew I would have to quit the house if I wanted to do anything and so I came home from work, had lunch, picked up the novel I was translating, took sharpened pencils and paper to Groppi, and worked in the comfortable air-conditioned tearoom from 3 o'clock until 7. At 7 o'clock I went home, ate dinner, and went to bed. This is how I was able to translate all of these books. I loved them and relished every minute I could spend in the worlds and adventures of Arsene Lupin and Sherlock Holmes!" And, indeed, he was a prodigious translator, though he took liberties with the novels, sometimes altering them or condensing them. I shall always be grateful to translators for making such books accessible to young Egyptian readers who, like myself, lost themselves in them. I remember buying the first of these in a pocketbook edition for a piaster. After the first taste, I was hooked. These volumes were published by Omar Abd al Aziz Amin, himself a fine translator.

In the early 1950s I was admitted to the university and my father decided it was time to move back to Cairo. He found an apartment in a building in Roda, close to the Nile. It was airy and had lots of trees around it. At that time apartments were easy to find and rents cheap, unlike today when people who are ready to marry and start a family have to hold off because they cannot find affordable housing. In any case, this apartment was spacious even though the kitchen and bathroom were small and pretty basic. The family room was much used and the furniture showed it, whereas the parlor, which was furnished more formally and was also called the "salon," was held in pristine condition and kept shuttered except when we had guests. At the far end of the apartment, on either side of a long hallway, we had three bedrooms, one for parents, one for boys and the other for girls. The apartment, like all the others in the building, had two balconies that we enjoyed a lot. For us children, being in Cairo during this period of social change was a source of great excitement. I started university filled with hope, studied diligently, and spent evenings at Café Riche or Ali Baba—coffeehouses where the intellectual youth of my day gathered and where the now famous Egyptian novelist Naguib Mahfouz often came. Tables and chairs spilled out onto the sidewalks and street overlooking Tahrir Square, steps from the Egyptian Museum of Antiquities. It was an exciting time full of nationalistic fervor, heated discussion, and hope.

One night I was returning home late, planning to take the last bus to Roda from Tahrir Square, when I ran into my Helwan school buddy. His uncle, the Islamic fundamentalist, had ramped up his activities and was attracting government attention. The authorities feared his influence and were watching him and his family. Soon they would be arrested. That night, however, my friend stood at the bus stop, looking lost and dejected. I expressed surprise at seeing him in Cairo, we embraced, and I asked him what he was doing standing there. He explained about his relatives and said, "I don't know where to go. Do me a favor and take me home with you tonight." I said, "Take you home with me? How can I do this? My house is not ready for a guest." He explained that he could not go home. He suspected his family members were in danger, soon to be rounded up as dissidents. As he was now a lawyer, they had told him that he must stay free in order to defend them. I was surprised by his request and very apprehensive about the consequences of taking him home.

The bonds of loyalty prevailed, however, and I said, "I'll take you home with me." When we got to the apartment, it was quiet, my parents and siblings asleep. I pointed him in the direction of my room and told him to make himself comfortable, that I would be back. I roused my brother and warned him, saying, "So and so is with me. He'll be sleeping in my room," after which I went to the kitchen and saw that there was food I could heat. I offered him dinner, but he refused. So I made tea, we drank it and went to sleep. When I woke at dawn, he was gone. The newspapers that morning were full of the news of this family. His uncle, two other male family members, two aunts, and two of his siblings had been arrested in their home the night before. My friend never forgot that I had offered him shelter that night, thus sparing him arrest. I could not do otherwise, as I believe in the rules of *shahaama*, and in this respect I am closer in spirit to the culture of Upper Egypt, the Saeed, than I am to that of Lower Egypt. In the south people are proud and have preserved traditions and observed them. And what is this *shahaama*? It is doing good with no reward expected. It is readiness to offer help, even to a stranger. It is acknowledging good deeds. It is being loyal and not trading in others people's secrets. *Shahaama* defines and perpetuates certain values and is its own reward. This is how I have understood it.

One other student made a vivid impression on me and to this day I read about his activities in the newspapers as a leader of the Sudanese Muslim Brotherhood. When he came to Egypt as a student, the Egyptian government was granting many scholarships to our southern brothers. He was one of many whom Egypt embraced and educated. We became friends, took walks on the Nile, discussed politics, literature, the news, whatever young men talk about. Years later, when I went to the Sudan and called on him, his reception was frigid. Friendship could no longer bridge our religious, nor even perhaps our ethnic, differences.

From the time I was an adolescent, I dreamed of becoming a writer. Instead, I became a teacher, but I also wrote, contributing my first articles to *Al Kutla*. Mr. Makram Ebayd was the founder of this magazine, a project he undertook after he broke away from the Wafd Party (*Hizb al Wafd*), a nationalist liberal party founded in 1919 and dissolved in 1952. He had been a member in good standing until irreconcilable differences between him and Nahas Pasha and his wife, the influential Zaynab al Nahas, made it impossible for him to remain.

At the time all this was happening, I became involved in cultural and political activity. These were outlets for a young man in a socially and sexually repressive society. I offered articles on the psychology of revolution to *Al Masri*, a newspaper that featured the weekly column "Books for Everyone," but the editor turned me down. He was not interested in the subject. And what did he feature instead? A book about King Farouk and his relationships with women. I was fired up about the nascent revolution and he chose gossip to sell papers. What to do? I looked to my role models for guidance.

One of my role models was Muhammad Ahmad Khalafallah, who wrote on the art of storytelling in the Qur'an and whom Muslim fundamentalists accused of being an atheist. He responded to their accusation in a piece published in the most popular Egyptian daily, *Al Ahram*, claiming that in the Holy Qur'an itself there was an injunction forbidding a believer or any other from calling another "atheist."

Dr. Youssef Murad, a professor who introduced integrative psychology to Egypt and founded the Takaamuliyya School, was also a role model. I attended as many of his lectures as I could. Another was the late Sheikh Amin al Kholy, a Muslim cleric who was, for a time, the head of Arabic Studies at Cairo University. I also attended talks by Salah Abd al Sabbour, Farouk Khorshed, and the well-known Islamic poetess Aysha Abd al Rahmaan.

She called herself *Bint el Nile*, Daughter of the Nile. She was a native of Damietta in the Delta, a student of Amin al Kholy, and became his second wife.

Another man I deeply admired was Salama Moussa. I went to his lectures at the Cairo YMCA in 1945 and 1946, and as I came to know him he became my ideal of an intellectual. I admired his intellectual courage, his liberal views, and his efforts to modernize Egypt. He warned against blindly following tradition, saying, "Question everything!" I still cherish my copy of his memoir, *The Autobiography of Salama Moussa.*

Twice I attended Abbas Mahmud al 'Akkad's weekly meetings given at his home in Heliopolis. He was one of the founders of Al Madrasa al Gadeeda, the New School. The other two founders were Ibrahim Abd al Kader al Mazni and the poet Abd al Rahman Shukri. Dr. Akkad wrote not only on literature but also on history and politics. I followed him closely until, in one of his lectures one day, he said that women were physically, morally, and intellectually inferior to men. Instantly, I took a vivid dislike to this man. I noted that with him, there was no room for discussion. At some point in his lecture series, he launched an attack on the precepts of socialism, clearly expecting his audience to sit rapt, listen, and not question his premises. There was something vindictive about the man that became clear at the time of his vitriolic assault on Salama Moussa. When Salama Moussa advocated for public services to meet the needs of the people, including his nationwide campaign to build public toilets for the new Egypt, al 'Akkad took to calling him "that toilet man." I was disgusted and stopped attending his lectures. I must confess that though Salama Moussa was one of my intellectual heroes, I was disappointed in him when his responses to al 'Akkad fell into the same quagmire and he called al 'Akkaad a mulatto who denied his roots and tried to pass for white—Turkish, as a matter of fact. The Turks having ruled Egypt, they were both hated and admired. Salama Moussa's comment reflected Egypt's complex dance with race, whereby whiter came to be considered as better. I grew wary of these debates and saw that their tenor mirrored the moral climate of the nation. I wanted to get out and began to think of emigration. However, it would be years before I could leave Egypt for good, as my time for change had not yet ripened into a reality.

I graduated from Cairo University with a bachelor of arts degree in the top 10 percent of my class and decided to register for the master's degree program. The professor who interviewed me put every possible obstacle in my way, however. In this case, it was a question of religious discrimination. He was a known Muslim fanatic and did not want a single Christian in the program. Although he could not outright deny me entrance into the program, he made impossible demands, giving me fifty books to read and be examined on, some of them in medieval French. He said, "When you have studied these, Nader, come back and see me and I'll test you. If you pass, then you can register for the master's degree program." Of course, I could see that students with lower scores were getting into the program and I knew that they had not had to meet similar requirements. I went back to see him and said, "I am refusing to consider your unrealistic demands, sir." His response was, "In that case, you cannot register." I wrote and submitted a grievance against him that eighteen others signed. It was not until 1952, however, with the dawning of the Egyptian revolution and the formation of what were called purging committees, that he was dismissed on the basis of systematic discrimination.

In 1953 I applied to the Ministry of Education, hoping to get a teaching post, and was assigned to a school in Giza. I had been there only three months when the principle of my school came to my classroom and asked me to step outside for a moment. In a worried whisper, he asked, "What have you done? The purging committee is asking for you." I said, "I think I know what this is about." He said, "Go and see. I'll take over your class." I went. The committee met on the campus of Cairo University. They asked me to report on the professor in question, on his professional conduct. Why had I submitted a grievance? I said, "He has students kiss his hand and asks the impossible as a way to discriminate against some of us when it suits him." I explained about the reading list, saying, "And if this is what is required to register for graduate school, what will be required to write the dissertation?" The spokesman for the committee simply asked, "What is it you wish?" I said, "To be permitted to apply for graduate school and study for a master's degree." The response was, "Consider it done." This is how the professor was fired and how I began my graduate studies.

My personal evolution was not only moral, spiritual, and intellectual, but also physical. I learned to endure. When I completed the master's degree I was assigned to teach in Qena and dreaded returning there, but had no choice. As a youngster in Qena I had the support of my family, but now would be on my own, and I began to look for company along with lodgings. Other teachers in Qena recommended a hotel managed by a Greek named Pano. The hotel itself dated back to 1900 and many teachers rented rooms there. I did the same. We were bachelors and therefore were never invited to private homes for fear we might impinge on family sanctity, particularly when there were daughters in residence. In my loneliness, I took to drinking and smoking. Some of my colleagues turned to religion, others to drugs.

I soon realized that I was taking a bad direction and decided to channel my energies into something constructive instead. I conceived of and produced a school magazine that I hand printed, turning out a hundred copies at a time. It was short lived, however. In the sixth issue, I wrote an editorial entitled

"Turn on the Lights," a piece in praise of the revered blind writer and nationalist Taha Hussein, especially his advocacy of education for all Egyptians. He had said that it should be as free as air and water. After the magazine was distributed, I was called into the mayor's office, accused of communist leanings, and ordered to stop printing and to stop using school property to launch my propaganda. I went to the school principle, a great man who had taught at the University of Baghdad before returning to Egypt. He said, "Don't worry, 'Ustaz Nader, we know who you are and you are no communist." But his endorsement was really no more than a consolation. He wielded no clout and I could not go against orders without losing my job or worse. It was clear to me that every creative endeavor was met with a challenge and that few wanted to see others succeed. This mean-spiritedness permeated the nation. In my discouragement, I turned to drinking brandy again.

A group of town notables, calling themselves the Qena Cultural Club, met in the lobby of the hotel where I lived to drink and gamble until 4 or 5 in the morning, leaning on each other as they left, slurring their speech, and laughing inappropriately as they wove their way home. I joined briefly and soon realized my error. I had to get out of this environment and bring balance back into my life. As I could not ask for a leave of absence, and vacation days for feasts were too short for me to travel the long distance home, I put in for sick leave. Giving the school doctor a few pounds to sign me out, I got on the train to Cairo and there, with the support and love of family and good friends, I was able to right myself.

When I returned to Qena to finish out the year, I kept away from the so-called Qena Cultural Club. I stopped drinking and turned to books for solace, resolving to leave Qena as soon as possible. It was a desert. Even my service as a teacher was hampered by impossible restrictions. Thankfully, I was rescued from

Qena by a friend of my father's who put a good word in for me at the Ministry of Education. I was assigned to a school in Cairo, in Giza, not far from where my family lived.

I would like to go back to the summer of 1952 when I had an interesting experience and was once again accused of communism. I was delegated to a youth camp on the western coast of Egypt, in the town of Marsa Matruh. These camps, created after the revolution in order to give youngsters a chance to live in a healthy environment, were part of a movement toward a new Egypt and the push for greater opportunities for all. These youngsters lived in tents by the sea, eating well, drinking well, engaging in sports, learning. I was in charge of cultural programming.

I had prepared a series of lectures about liberty and justice for all, about equality and building a democracy together, and delivered them to the campers in Marsa Matruh. Once again, I was accused of communist leanings. How could this be? Well, at camp, members of the Muslim Brotherhood did not like my views. The camp director called me in and said, "Don't you know that you must take into consideration our conservative and traditionally sensitive students?" I said, "What do you mean? I am traditional too. What have I said that could be interpreted as subversive? Have I been involved in a scandal?" He said, "No, no, Mr. Nader, it's just that the views you espouse are too liberal for some of our students. You must be more sensitive." I said, "If you wish, I will leave for Cairo by the next train." He protested, "No, no, no, this is not at all what I intended." I said, "I must have freedom of speech, or resign. The Muslim Brothers can enter into discussion with the rest of the group and I can arrange for them to express their opinions openly. Why must they go behind my back to complain? Let them schedule a presentation directly with me and I will announce it at camp meeting." He agreed, but nothing came of this.

After the revolution, the challenge facing the nation was whether we could have a democratic form of government and a multiparty system, or whether the revolutionary council would remain in power. There were fundamental differences between Mohammad Naguib, the nation's first president, and Gamal Abdel Nasser, who became its second. The old parties supported Naguib, whereas the army and the group calling themselves the Free Officers supported 'Abdel Nasser. They clearly had every intention of rising to the top along with him. Watching this unfold, my great fear was that power would corrupt good intentions. Time proved me right.

Although I was in favor of a republic and did not support the monarchy, what I saw was a dictatorship. I had read Kimball Young's book on social psychology and applied his framework to analyze Nasser's revolution. I concluded that it was a coup rather than a revolution. I could not see how a change was going to take place, nor could I see myself continuing as I was. There was an atmosphere of distrust. I contemplated emigration.

I applied for immigrant status to Brazil and to Australia. Neither worked out for me. At the Brazilian consulate the interviewer asked if I spoke Portuguese. I did not. He said, "You are a teacher. Are you ready to work as a laborer in Brazil while you learn the language?" I was not.

I took my papers to the Australian consulate, filled out applications, and waited. A year later I was cleared. I presented myself at the consulate and asked what kind of work I could expect to find with my education and experience. I was told I could probably start out as a janitor in a church or a clerk somewhere. I was shocked and left. I didn't have a clue at the time that it was perfectly fine to take any sort of work to get a foot in the door and that in such societies there was no shame in doing so. I had been a civil servant in Egypt, assured a job upon graduation, and received a salary at the end of the month no matter how I performed. This was the mentality instilled in me. I wanted the title that went with my degree, and if I worked half of the year and decided to be a slacker the other half, I could get sick leave, summer leave, formal leave, leave to grieve, family leave, any sort of leave and fit right in with the way the system worked. I am ashamed to say I followed the crowd in this respect and I hated myself for it. I decided I must do something to change and this included leaving Egypt.

When my first two choices for emigration failed, I applied for a teaching position in the Sudan, where there was a Coptic school, an Anglican school, and an Egyptian secondary school in the city of Khartoum. First, I had to sit for a series of exams. These were on Sudanese history and various other cultural topics that I first had to study. I studied, passed the exams, and was then interviewed about interests, readings, and my approach to teaching. I was asked what were my strongest subjects and also my hobbies. One examiner asked, "What encyclopedias are you familiar with?" I mentioned a few, including the one I had first come in contact with, *The Encyclopedia Britannica*. I even mentioned some that the examiner himself was not aware of. He was satisfied with my answers.

I had read *The African Giant* by Basil Davidson, a British Africanist, and had educated myself about social and political movements in the Sudan, Nigeria, Ghana, Guinea, and other African nations. I was especially interested in how these nations achieved independence. Reading was my chief hobby and my professional obligation to my students was to stay well informed. I made sure I did.

After I passed the exams and satisfied the interviewers, I was assigned to a school in Port Sudan. This was a poor city on the Red Sea, where the heat was extreme and the humidity 90 percent nine months of the year. I feared it would not be a healthy environment for me, chiefly because of the climate but also because I had heard that it was, like Qena, a hardship post. I was in a quandary as to what to do. I was already in the Sudan and so went to see the head of the Egyptian mission to the Sudan, who was, as it turned out, a very decent gentleman. I shared my concerns with him and my reticence about Port Sudan. At first he said, "Well, I can send you back to Cairo." I answered that I was eager to stay in the Sudan but would appreciate it if he would consider posting me somewhere other than Port Sudan. I knew there were openings. I said, "Sir, I have heard that there are positions open in Khartoum." He paused and then answered, "Wait a few days. I'll see what I can do." A week later, he called me in and offered me a position at the Anglican high school in Khartoum. I thanked him and said I was glad to be assigned there since I had some experience with Protestants from my father's association with the Plymouth Brotherhood. My English had also improved and I felt I could do my job well.

As soon as I knew where I would be teaching, I looked for housing and found a furnished room in the home of an elderly Greek lady who was very kind. She offered breakfast and lunch with the room, and I accepted. A lot of Greeks had found opportunity in the Sudan but had left after independence. It was lonely for her, as there was almost no Greek community left to speak of. I asked her why she stayed when members of her family had left, and she explained that the Sudan had been her home with her late husband, that she had lived there all of her life and would die there.

From the start in Khartoum, I was active in the Arab Egyptian Club and was elected to its board. The club's building served as a gathering place for Egyptians employed in the Sudan. There was a cafeteria where we could get two meals a day, a recreation hall, and meeting rooms. I started a lecture series there and offered my services. I talked on African independence movements and my lectures were well attended. That year, I met the Sudanese poet Muhammad al Fayturi as well as Dr. Abd al Hamid Saleh, who became a minister in President Numairi's cabinet. I also became acquainted with Dr. Ezzedine Amer, who was married to an Englishwoman and later had to flee to Britain to avoid being arrested by Numairi. These were all unusual and interesting people who played a part in my intellectual life in the Sudan.

Although I had an active intellectual and professional life in the Sudan, there were no opportunities to socialize and female companionship was nonexistent. How different this was from my time in Helwan and Cairo, where I had enjoyed friendship and conversation with the opposite sex and had particularly appreciated getting acquainted with a feminine point of view on life beyond that of my mother and sisters.

During my time in the Sudan, though I occupied myself fully, I missed the company of my mother and sisters. One day, a telegram came that affected every part of my life. My mother had died. I was full of remorse at not having been with her and sick with grief. I requested a leave of absence and returned to Egypt to be with my father and siblings. To this day I ache when I think that I missed her last days.

At home, I contacted Dr. Khalafallah and went to see him about getting reassigned to Cairo. I was seeking a job with the Ministry of Culture. He agreed to help and introduced me to Dr. Abd al Aziz al Ahwaany, a professor of literature at Cairo University. The Ministry of Culture was then located in Heliopolis. This was during the years of the union between Egypt and Syria. After interviewing me for an hour, he agreed to my transfer from the Ministry of Education to the Ministry of Culture and wrote a letter to the minister of education requesting my transfer. My joy at this new prospect did not last 48 hours, however, as the unity between Syria and Egypt was dissolved and new people appointed to the ministry. Any decisions taken by the old guard were declared invalid and so was my transfer, and I was thus returned to the Ministry of Education. Though I asked Dr. Khalafallah to intercede on my behalf, he said there was nothing he could do. So I buried myself in my work and in books. I read al Jabarti, Ibn Iyas, and contemporaries like Mahfouz. I took pleasure in my visits to bookstores and acquired every new book by Mahfouz as soon as it was published. I have a complete collection of first editions of his novels. Reading, which had always been my solace, continued to sustain and nurture me.

A year went by and I was surprised to hear again from Dr. Khalafallah. He telephoned and invited me to come see him. When I went, he said, "Would you like to work on a new magazine for the Ministry of Culture, Nader?" He had returned to the Ministry of Culture and once again had some influence. I gladly agreed, of course, and began to write for a magazine on culture called *Magallat al Saqaafa*. I was now teaching at a secondary school in Giza and continued to do so. I worked on the magazine for two full years, but resigned when arguments and petty squabbling between contributors and editorial staff led to deep discord, quelling creative energy and diminishing productivity. There was no pleasure in being there.

Soon after I resigned, I offered my services as a translator to the Franklin Book Program, headed by Dr. Zaki Naguib Mahmud. My first assignment was to translate a book on Christopher Columbus. It would seem that the fates were giving me a glimpse of new horizons, of America. I applied for a visa to the United States and finally got it. I said a month-long goodbye to my family and friends, packed, and sailed to New York from Port Said on board a freighter belonging to the Holland America Line. It carried only two-dozen passengers and made the crossing in twenty-one days. My family came with me to Port Said, tears were shed and good wishes offered, and thus began the final chapter of my life, which has been one of the best as well as one of the happiest.

I left Egypt with $200 in my pocket, my personal belongings, and a few books. I also carried close to my person a cross that belonged to my mother and that I have kept near me all these years. This cross was a symbol of her Christianity and her devotion to the Coptic Church. I feel protected by it to this day, as it is a physical symbol of her faith and mine and carries with it her blessings.

When I landed in New York, I stayed with an Egyptian acquaintance, a fellow I had gone to school with and who had emigrated two years before me. He had a degree in chemistry and worked in a medical lab in Queens. I very quickly began to look for work, first naively going to an employment agency that turned out to be for sailors looking to ship out. I can still hear the laughter that ushered me out of that place. I then tried a number of other avenues, finally applying to a university library, which would have been the logical place to start. As a new immigrant, one is often disoriented and uncertain of what direction to take. At the library, my knowledge of Arabic and my work as a translator, teacher, and writer served to recommend me. I was hired on as a cataloguer and given the opportunity of a lifetime to continue my education. I registered in a work-study program, took classes to qualify for graduate school, and eventually earned a master's degree in education and Arabic Studies. Of course, as soon as I got my first paycheck, I rented a small apartment and learned to cook and to rely on myself in every way. Long gone were the days when I had burned vegetables on my mother's Primus stove!

These New York years were ones of struggle and satisfying accomplishment, and thus of happiness. I was going somewhere and I felt that nothing could hold me back in this new land I was eager to adopt wholeheartedly. I reached a high point when I met my wife Elizabeth, who was then a graduate student. There was an instant spark between us. We courted for two years before becoming engaged and married a year later. She was from a conservative family of Protestant ministers, some of whom had actually spent time in my hometown of Assiut. We were drawn to each other by common interests, and our conservative values helped to cement our relationship. Elizabeth had visited one of her uncles in Assiut after she graduated from high school and had wonderful memories of her time in Egypt. This was a topic of conversation that gave us pleasure in the early days of our courtship. When I asked her to marry me, she honored me by accepting, and we began our life together, deciding to leave New York. We were lucky enough to find teaching jobs in the Midwest and an apartment we could rent. We liked our new location and purchased a house and began a family. Elizabeth worked part time after our first child was born and did not go back to full-time teaching until all three of our children were in school. Our children are now grown and married and have families of their own. Over time, Elizabeth and I sponsored my brother, two nephews, and a niece to come to the United States. They have done well for themselves and provide us with a touch of Egypt when we all get together. None of us have forsaken our Egyptian roots, but I can say with utmost sincerity that America has truly been for us all a land of opportunity and happiness.

The childhood memories I carry with me as I age are the priceless cornerstones of my life. The subsequent struggles and accomplishments are the building blocks that have formed the edifice of our lives. My wife is the crown on it and our children the jewels as she and I move into our golden years together. I am grateful for all that has come to pass and for all that remains unknown. And so this is my story to date with all of its textures, rough and smooth. I have told it to you as truthfully as I could. It is my story and in a small way it is also a story of Egypt.

Youssef Salman

Both of my parents were born in Alexandria. I don't know how they met, perhaps in the course of Jewish youth gatherings or maybe their marriage was arranged. In any case, they considered themselves Egyptian, although their own parents had come from North Africa. My father's father was a merchant, rather a simple man who came from Algeria. My mother's father was from Morocco, from Meknes. I never met my grandparents, since they were dead by the time I was born, but my older sisters did.

My father and mother had a limited education. They went to the Jewish school in Alexandria around 1910. Mother tutored refugees at some point before graduating, but I never found out where these refugees came from. No doubt they were other Jews. She was proud of this period in her life.

So many people from so many places sought refuge in Egypt before and after the First World War. It was a kind and gentle place, really. It had perfect weather and generous people who opened their doors and accepted others readily. Egypt was a land of opportunity for those who knew how to advance themselves. You could live very well in Egypt and a large Jewish community did. There were also Europeans, Croatians, Greeks, Armenians, Italians, and White Russians. I was told that Mademoiselle Eudoxie Kutuzov, the grandniece of Field Marshal Kutuzov, who drove Napoleon's army out of Russia, lived in Alexandria. When the Bolsheviks took over, her family fled and settled in Egypt. So many people came and would have stayed had the political climate not changed. I don't think I would have, but then I was not given a choice. I was expelled from Egypt because of my Zionist activities. Later, others left because they were Jews and the government did not want them and seized their properties.

I'm not sure I ever felt as much at home in Egypt as my parents did, probably because I did not really learn Arabic and was educated in foreign-language schools. Also, although I was born in Egypt, I am a Zionist and above all a Jew, and I felt my future lay elsewhere.

My mother, having a primary school education, taught for a short time and was very proud of this. She brought it up frequently, boasting that she was the advanced one in her family. Primary school education prepared you much better than it does today, and many became teachers with only a primary school education. After she married, however, mother became a full-time homemaker and raised six girls and me, her youngest and only son. She always said that as I was her seventh child, I was her lucky charm. She called me Youssef, although on my birth certificate I am Asher Youssef Salman. She said I was a pearl come to brighten her old age and compared herself to Sarah, who had her son Isaac when she was ninety and her husband Abraham was one hundred years old. Of course, mother was only in her forties and compared herself to the biblical matron for effect, but she also liked it when people teased her, saying, "Oh, Ashira, you are young enough to bear another tribe of children!" The name Asher was chosen for me because it means happy and sounds like my mother's own name.

My father was in the textile business. He bought wholesale and sold retail. At that time, it was difficult for Arabs to go directly to a big importer, so businessmen like my father were often the go-between. There were whole streets in Alexandria where textile merchants plied their trade, rows of stores selling nothing but cloth. In addition to imported textiles like tweed from England and linen from Italy, Egyptian textile mills in Kafr al Dawwar, Mehalla al Kubra, and other towns produced high-quality cotton, silk, and wool. My father started as a common clerk in one of the stores in the textile district. He became a salesman for a time and then bought his own business, which he passed on to me. As a salesman, he traveled to Mansoura, Kafr al Zayyat, Damanhur, and throughout the Delta region of Egypt taking orders from retailers and selling to them in bulk.

At home we spoke French, as Arabic was considered the language of the common people and the Jews held themselves a notch above. Arabic was for the serving class, the masses. We were better and spoke it only to the maid. Yet Arabic was the first language of my parents and they felt most comfortable speaking it. We, their children, could understand and speak Arabic, but did not read or write it and did not want to. We prided ourselves on speaking French, English, Italian, Greek, anything but Arabic. We were snobs about European culture and only wanted to be European even though we had been born and lived in Egypt.

I went to the École Jabes in Camp Cesar, a short tramway ride from where we lived in the Ibrahimiyya district of Alexandria. The school was small and well regarded, a private school with classes conducted in French. It was founded by the Jabes family, a prominent Jewish family in Alexandria. My sisters went there too. When I received my Certificat d'études primaires, my parents transferred me to an English school. They reasoned that English would be more useful to me as a boy, as it was the language of business. They sent me to Saint Andrew's Mission, a Scottish Christian missionary school whose mission it was to convert Jewish kids to Christianity and Coptic kids to Protestantism. They could not touch the Muslim kids, however, because it was illegal to proselytize among the Muslims; the school would have been promptly shut down if they had. Muslim boys and other boys from the upper classes attended Victoria College and upper-class girls went to Notre Dame de Sion, a Catholic school where they were taught by nuns. Some were day students and others boarders. So there were few Muslims at the Scottish school and fewer still at École Jabes.

The Scottish Mission school staff enticed us to attend Sunday school and church by giving us sweets and free food. In the office of the headmaster hung this sign: TO THE JEW, FIRST. I suspect it meant, "first, convert the Jew." This message fell on deaf ears with us since Jews are a committed lot and we stuck together and were neither interested in deviating from our faith nor our community. My friends at the École Jabes were all Jews, as were my friends at the Scottish Mission School. There were Greeks and Armenians there too, but the Armenian kids, who were as smart or smarter and certainly as competitive as the Jewish kids, also pretty much stuck together. We all tended to stick with our own groups; birds of a feather and all that.

I was turning sixteen when the Second World War broke out. I had just taken my exams for the London Chamber of Commerce. Exams were mailed to England for correction and the results were mailed back. But mine were mailed just before war broke out and communications were severed. We never got back the results, but the training and the language skills that were taught ultimately served me well.

The summer of 1940, I was getting ready to go on vacation when the headmaster at École Jabes telephoned my father at work, as we had no telephone at home. He said, "I know of a job at a firm of chartered accountants and I put forward your son's name for the job. If he is interested, he should apply promptly." My father told me and I immediately put away my bathing suit, went to the firm, and was hired on the spot. My starting salary was 3 Egyptian pounds a month and I worked from 9 until 1, went home for lunch and a nap, and returned to work in the evening for another few hours. This was the customary schedule for most businesses and shops. Three pounds was good money at the time, as everything was cheap. We lived very well in Egypt.

I especially remember how pleasant summer days were. We ate a late lunch, enjoyed a siesta, got up for afternoon tea, went to work, and came home for a light dinner. Sometimes we had visitors, and on weekends we went to the Alexandria Sporting Club. We just called it "Sporting." We also rented cabanas (we called them "cabins") at Rushdi or Stanley Bay, some of the nicer Alexandria beaches on the Mediterranean. We gathered there to socialize or visited one another's homes. We would have a drink and play cards or *tawla* (backgammon), at which I excelled. Card games were for small change and *conqin*, an early form of rummy, was a favorite.

At the age of twenty-two, I went into business with my father. It was a satisfying experience. We went to the beach less and less and worked more and more, aiming to move up in the world. A couple of my sisters worked also, whereas the others married and had children. When I left Egypt, they followed. My parents, however, refused to leave.

In the mid-1940s, I began to get involved in Zionist activities. My family was unaware that I belonged to a Zionist club. They had no clue that I regularly attended meetings and worked undercover to send boys and girls to Palestine. We falsified passports, forged visas, or got British visas that allowed us entry into Palestine. We all had code names and mine was Samuel.

On the morning of May 15, 1948, an officer of the Egyptian police attended by two *shaweesh* (soldiers) knocked on our door. My mother answered. The officer said, "We are here to arrest one called Samuel." My mother said, "There is no Samuel here, *ya Bey*," using this term of respect for the officer. But, I stepped forward and revealed my identity. Had the officer searched my room, he would have found a radio used to communicate with our counterparts in Palestine and equipment to forge the passports and visas. There was no violence, but a lot of illegal activity. We didn't know all that much and a lot of our activities were cloak-and-dagger stuff, really. We were committed but pretty innocent. I was in my twenties and excited at the thought of being arrested like others of my Zionist buddies. In my room I had hidden the forging equipment and the radio, but left some telltale rubber stamps on my desk. I didn't want my parents harmed if these were found, and so I asked the officer to let me go to the bathroom. They let me go, and I hid everything and got a message out to one of my pals about where to look for the equipment. I then followed the officer. My mother wailed and slapped her cheeks over and over, saying, "What have you done, Youssef?! What have you done?!" I did my best to comfort her before being led away to what they called a detention camp. It was nothing like in Europe and the horrors of German concentration camps. This camp was at Abu Qir, on the Mediterranean. It was more like a Boy Scout camp than a detention camp. We were not really harmed and our Egyptian keepers were good natured and accommodating. Actually, our guards were *masakeen*, poor fellows, guileless really. They were grateful for anything we gave them and thanked us sincerely when we shared food and supplies sent by our families. They were happy to get anything at all, even the government rations dispensed to detainees like the Muslim Brothers, the communists, and other rabble-rousers. There was no physical abuse whatsoever. In fact, the atmosphere was that of an open-air resort. Some of our fellow detainees did go a little crazy because, after all, we didn't know what lay ahead. Some allowed their fears to get the better of them whereas the rest of us took our predicament in stride. Life went on as usual, just in a different setting. We were friendly with one another and we had good relationships with the guards. We often had political discussions, bantered, laughed, and joked. On the street this random group of people might have been strangers, but at the camp we were brothers.

I befriended an officer by the name of Abu Taleb. He had a newborn son he was very proud of named Taleb, so we called him Father of Taleb rather than using his given name. It was a courtesy and a traditional Egyptian way of addressing someone like him. He came on the third and last shift of the day and I spoke to him in Arabic from the start. He was genuinely pleased: *"Bi tifham arabi"* (You understand Arabic)? *"B'tit kallim arabi"* (You speak Arabic)? To him, it was a sign that I cared about Egypt and this endeared me to him. To him I was a foreigner, even though I was born in Egypt. *"Bi yet kallim Arabi"* (he speaks Arabic), he would tell the other guards, and this pleased them. It didn't take much to please them. Egyptians are good-hearted and a little honey goes a long way with them.

We were allowed to send one letter per week to our families. I never sent one through the camp machine because they were censored. I smuggled them out with a friendly guard like Abu Taleb. One time, I gave a letter to Abu Taleb. It was addressed to my father, not at home but at his place of business. Abu Taleb went to the post office, bought a stamp, and sent the letter. There was starting to be a lot of sequestration and seizing of property, and unbeknownst to me, our company had been sequestered. A government trustee was in charge and the letter never made it past his desk. He opened it. There was really nothing of consequence in the letter other than reassurances to my parents to cheer them up. I added a postscript saying that I had found a way to smuggle bottles of wine into the camp and that we were planning to cook coq au vin. The trustee reported our activities to the military governor of Alexandria, who summoned the head of the camp for questioning and rebuked him:

"Is this what is going on in your camp, Sir?!" The head of the camp was unaware and genuinely surprised. He questioned us and the guards, and when it was my turn I saw my letter on his desk. "Did you write this?" he asked. I said I had. "What do you mean you are drinking wine in the camp?" he asked. I answered, "Commander, wine and spirits are forbidden, but I tell my parents these things to ease their minds and reassure them that I am well taken care of here." He seemed satisfied but also asked, "How did you mail this letter?" It did not have the censor's stamp on it, so he knew. "I gave it to a soldier, your excellency." He asked, "Who is the soldier? What is his name?" I decided to play the fool and said, "He had just come out of our bathroom, Sir, and I didn't look closely at him." The officer said, "Soldiers are forbidden to use your bathroom, don't you know this?" I said, "You tell them, Sir." "When was this?" he persisted, and I said, "It was either Wednesday or Thursday." "What time? Which shift?" he asked, trying to get me to falter. I said, "The one that starts between four and six in the afternoon, Excellency." He called me a liar and the next day brought me out to identify the soldier in a lineup. These boys are poor *fellaheen* (peasants), and they were scared to death. I looked them over and said, "He's not here, Sir." For weeks afterward these soldiers loved me, saying, "This foreigner, this *khawaga*, is a *shahm*." In other words, I had acted with honor, *shahaama*.

When Abu Taleb came on duty, I said to him, "Did you think I would betray you?" He answered, "You have the *shahaama* of a *Saidi* (of an Upper Egyptian). I knew you would not harm a hair on Taleb's little head by betraying his father!"

We had smuggled a camera into the camp. There were six ringleaders who took pictures. We had been in camp almost a year when a group from the *alam khususi*, Special Forces, something like the CIA, came to the camp. They announced that we would be liberated on one condition: we must leave Egypt. Israel and Egypt were in conflict, then they had a cease-fire, then again they were warring, and so it went, on again, off again. The Egyptians got tired of keeping us in the detention camps; it cost them money. They just wanted to be rid of us and so they asked, "Who wants to be liberated?" Of course everyone did. They said, "If you want your freedom, you will arrange to promptly leave the country." There was no deadline, really. They made it easy and so I left the camp on my own two feet, but I was faced with a grave problem. I had no passport. I had never applied for an Egyptian passport and now had to find a way to be admitted to another country. Finally, a family member convinced someone at the French consulate to issue me a laissez-passer, a document carried by someone of undetermined nationality allowing him entrance to another country. In my case, it was to Algeria. It bore my name, and after securing safe passage to Algeria, I applied for and got a French passport. My sisters followed suit but remained in Algeria after I left for France. On the day I was deported, I was allowed to see my parents and my sisters and to bid them farewell. I was taken in handcuffs to the port and ordered on board a ship sailing to Algiers. The handcuffs were symbolic at best, not secured to my wrists but left dangling on one of them.

Do you remember the smuggled camera? And the pictures the group of six took during our detention? Well, when we were liberated, these remained at camp. Somehow, Abu Taleb got a hold of the photos and brought them to the ship before it sailed. He distracted the soldiers who were in charge of me and gave me the pictures hidden inside a newspaper. I never saw him again, but I framed a few of the photos and have them on my desk. They remind me of the good time we had despite the circumstances. Also they remind me of the good-hearted Egyptians and of Abu Taleb, *shahaama*.

The years in Egypt were my formative years even though I lived at the heart of my Jewish community and continue to do so. I do remember the gentleness of the people of Egypt and how we were spared the horrors experienced by the Jews of Europe. I feel at home in France but cannot deny that Egypt welcomed us for a time.

Ali Kamal

My name is Ali Kamal and I was born in Cairo, Egypt, into a devout Muslim family. Some of my relatives achieved fame because of their role in the Muslim Brotherhood. My father and mother did not see eye to eye with these relatives even though they themselves were faithful Muslims and kept the tenets of Islam. They were traditional but open-minded, sending me as a little boy to a school run by nuns.

My father had a primary school education and was a self-made man. When he left school, he started working for a Jewish merchant who taught him a lot. Eventually he owned his own business, distributing electrical supplies. His shop was in the district of Ghamra, where in the 1920s he bought and sold land and built up some wealth this way. When he had sufficient resources saved up, he bought a piece of land in the district now called Ramsis, not far from the Cairo train station, and built a four-story apartment building with the top floor designated for his family and the lower floors as rental income.

My father kept his shop and continued to work there until his death. In fact, he died in his shop. As he was much older than my mother, she remained a widow for many years but was closely surrounded by her family, especially her children and grandchildren. I am sure that although she grieved for my father, she was otherwise fulfilled by the love of her family. She never appeared anything but calm, kind, and composed. Luckily, she preserved her good health and died in her sleep, having lived a good, long life.

My father's apartment building was completed in 1935 and I was born there a decade later. My oldest brother still lives there with his family, as does a sister who never married. I remember every detail of that apartment, as I was always an observant child and this quality has served me well as an adult, especially in my profession in the film industry as a production manager and documentary filmmaker.

In my youth, the streets around our apartment were in good repair and relatively quiet. People knew one another and extended greetings in the streets. These same streets are now so crowded and dilapidated that it is difficult to cross them without taking your life in your hands. If a car does not get you, a pothole might well do the job. One has to be cautious at every step. There is so much traffic, horns sounding, people moving day and night, coffee shops with radios blaring, that to survive this clamor one has to get used to it and cultivate inner peace. The mosque nearby is the same as it always was, and it is where I go for Friday prayers. The apartment buildings in the neighborhood have deteriorated too, as rents are controlled and are so low that landlords cannot afford to maintain their buildings in good repair. Rents are the same today as they were in 1935. Stairs that were once handsome and clean are now broken and covered in the dust of ages. Elevators are frozen in place and mute.

Ours was a middle-class neighborhood. It was pleasant. The apartment of my childhood, like so many others in the Ramsis district, was roomy and comfortable. It had three bedrooms, a bathroom, kitchen, family room, and what we called the "salon," which was used only when we had guests. The hallways of the apartment had floors made of cement tiles with marble chips worked into them. As a child, I loved to study these because the chips glittered and made patterns. I pretended they were fossilized animals or plants. Our family room was furnished simply with a couch and two chairs and a divan to one side for sitting or reclining.

Beyond the family room were the dining room and the very small kitchen. The dining room had a rectangular table with an oilcloth on top and a matching corner cupboard decorated with an inlay of flowers, where my mother kept glasses, dishes, and cutlery. Later, when refrigerators were available, my oldest brother bought one for the family and it was placed in the dining room. It was green and had a very shiny chrome handle that latched the door securely. The Frigidaire, as my mother called it, was off limits to children.

A balcony extended our living room and looked out onto the street. We spent a lot of time on this balcony as I was growing up, though now my brother keeps it closed against the incessant clamor of the city and the dust. As a child, however, it was sunny and pleasant, a great place for the family to gather and for us children to play. In winter, my mother sat out there to escape the chill of the apartment, which had high ceilings and was cold. Sitting in the sun, she picked rice or lentils in preparation for cooking lunch, trimmed vegetables, or sat quietly mending or drinking a glass of tea in the afternoon. In summer, the evening breezes were delightful on this balcony. There was the perfume of jasmine in the air, thanks to two potted star jasmines my mother loved and placed on either side of the balcony. A divan for sitting was pushed up against one wall and two wicker chairs with a table in between were across from it. We enjoyed wonderful summer nights there, as the air was clean and mild, cars were few, and Cairo was quieter.

My mother told the story of how I nearly tumbled off the balcony when I was five because my curiosity drew me to something going on in the street. My brother caught me by the leg, saving me from a fatal fall. I have vague recollections of the incident, of my tears and my mother's despairing of me and crying out: "Il walad dah hay Shayyebni" (This boy is going to make my hair turn prematurely white)! The kitchen too had a balcony. It was just big enough for two people to stand side by side. It faced a small alley, which was accessed from the street and onto which faced the tall, wrought-iron double doors of our building. As the neighborhood grew more crowded and more and more people acquired cars, this alley became a thorn in the side of building residents because people pulled in there at random and parked their cars, locked them, and left. Residents often found their own access blocked. Eventually, my brother put a thick padlocked chain across the alley and gave each resident a key to the lock. Now, when one of our cars is blocked by a neighbor's, we know which apartment door to knock on, and this solution has eliminated strangers' cars coming into the alley.

Three clotheslines stretched across the front of the kitchen balcony. They were strung on two dowels jutting out from the railings and were in constant use as our family grew. Dish towels, rags, children's clothing, and diapers were all hung there and only the main laundry of the house was hung on the rooftop. Did I mention that my oldest brother lived with us in the apartment with his wife and baby? He is the oldest of my parents' five children and he still lives there.

A basket on a very long rope hung from the banister of the kitchen balcony. I loved playing with it and could usually cajole my brother, Salah, into racing down the stairs to see if he could beat the basket's descent. He then placed something in the basket and raced back up. It was one of our games. If mother caught us at this game, she chided: "Get away from the edge of this balcony, Ali. And you, Salah, come back upstairs this instant!" And then she reminded us of my near fatal accident. The basket served a specific purpose, however. It was not a toy. It saved us having to go down to the street to buy produce from the ambulatory merchants plying their trade. It would be lowered to a street seller who filled it with a kilo or two of beans, tomatoes, cucumbers, onions, whatever my mother required of fresh vegetables. Garlic too was purchased in this manner and hung in braided ropes on the balcony summer and winter. Mother always inspected her purchases before sending money back down in the basket. I seem to remember that a year's supply of garlic was purchased at one time, but maybe it was periodically replenished, as we used a lot of it both fresh and in cooking. My parents believed it to be beneficial to health. Mother chopped it into cucumber or tomato salads and also into roasted, skinned eggplant cut in half and dressed with salt, coriander, chopped parsley, oil, and vinegar.

Dry goods were purchased by my father in bulk, as was fruit. In Egypt, it is often the men who buy fruit for the family. Male family members also bring gifts of seasonal fruit and like to be thought of as the ones who bring the best fruit. I can tell you that my uncle Salem always came to visit us in summer bringing a crate full of the largest and most fragrant mangoes we had ever seen or tasted, and uncle Salem's reputation was established as the one who knew where to purchase the best mangoes in Egypt. As he regularly traveled to Alexandria, he also brought, in season, the best figs grown in the western desert between Alexandria and Marsa Matruh. My father shopped weekly at 'Am Ahmad's fruit stand, just down the street from our house. 'Am Ahmad allowed him to pick and choose at will, not like other greengrocers who invariably sneaked a few pieces of rotten fruit with the sack just to tip the scales. When my mother spoke of these dishonest merchants to her sister, my aunt said, "But, Galila, he has to sell his stock, what else can the poor man do?" My aunt, everyone agreed, was so kind she was thought to be simpleminded, *tayyebah*. As to 'Am Ahmad, he reserved the best of what he had to sell for my father and my father paid a little extra for the favor.

I often wondered where 'Am Ahmad's overripe or rotting fruit went? Certainly not to our house.

My father brought home bananas and oranges in winter, guavas and dates in summer. We ate only fruits and vegetables in season. One fruit my father brought home from time to time because my mother loved it was *ishta* (cream), so called because of its creamy white interior and custardy texture. I too loved it and love it to this day. It is round or conical and greenish-blue in color and looks like a large pinecone with flesh as fragrant as jasmine. The flesh adheres to shiny black seeds and you suck it off. Like pomegranate, it yields little for the time spent eating it. But it is worth it. As a child, I washed and collected the seeds to play with, and one day, as an adult, I worked on a BBC production and wanted to tell the English crew about *ishta*. I could not name it, and so tried to describe it and also asked a friend who worked at the Ministry of Agriculture to write down the Latin name. He did: *Annona squamosa*. I brought a couple of sacks of the fruit to the English crew and one of them said, "Oh, mate, I know this, it's a sugar apple. They call it Sita's fruit in India!"

Streetsellers are a dying breed. A project I have in the back of my mind is a film about them. I'd like to record them before they all disappear. When I was a child, you could count on them coming by every day. Not so today. I remember the man who carried small earthenware pots of homemade yogurt on a round tray and sold them door to door, 1 piaster for three. My mother bought from him, although she made her own from buffalo milk. The milkman delivered door to door on his bicycle. He measured milk from two huge milk jars. They were made of aluminum, I think. He clanged his way down the street or up the stairs, calling, "*Laban, laban, ishta ya laban*" (Milk, milk, creamy milk)! The yogurt man collected his little brown pots when we were done but the milkman filled one of our own saucepans daily. The yogurt man I have not seen in years on any of the streets of Cairo. He became obsolete, no doubt, when yogurt became available in plastic tubs in grocery stores at competitive prices.

The *ful medammes* (fava bean) streetsellers, peddling their creamy strained *ful* sandwiches from wheeled carts, are still plentiful. They stand in one spot and you go to them. Likewise those who sell *kushari* (a dish of rice with lentils or noodles). In winter, some call out the virtues of their firebrand *hummus* (chickpeas), boiled, served in their own broth, dressed with salt, cayenne pepper, lime, the steaming brew poured into a tall, heavy glass for each customer. Other perambulating merchants sell yams on carts fitted with improvised oil-drum ovens. The yams bake as the merchant roams the streets tempting customers with his song of praise for the *batata*. One in our neighborhood recently sang out that his yams were sweet as sugar, delectable as chocolate: *Lazeeza ya batata, helwa ya chocolata* (yams as delicious as chocolate). It made me smile to hear him put a new twist, the chocolate, to a traditional call. But then Egyptians are like that, playful.

The streets were teeming with vendors going door to door when I was growing up. They carried their own scales and weights and their calls were poetry. You heard them praising their vegetables or fruits: my onions are the sweetest, my okra the freshest, my string beans the snappiest, my greens the greenest, my cabbages big as a full moon, my favas with summer still on their breath, and so on.

In our apartment was a small room, no more than a cubbyhole with a curtain across the opening, where the servant girl slept. She was not more than twelve or thirteen when she came to us, sent from our family's village in Minufiyya. There was no limit on the hours such children worked for meager wages collected at the end of the month by their fathers or an uncle. I remember Sakina, our little maid, had a ready smile and a song on the tip of her tongue despite her circumstances. My mother was kind to her, but Sakina also had a sweet disposition.

We lived on the top floor of the building. Above us was the *sitooh*, the rooftop, which had storage and utility rooms and a laundry room with a cold water spigot. Water was heated on a Primus stove and the washing done in the *karawana*, a round, shallow, tinned-copper washtub. The whites were boiled and everything was dried on the laundry lines after they had been wiped down.

Father rented the apartments below us, one to a cousin and his family, another to my mother's sister and her family, and a third to a Muslim cleric who taught at Al Azhar University. He was a big, kindly man with a limp. His wife and daughters, however, were quarrelsome, and sometimes we heard their voices raised in argument or making demands. The youngest child in this family was a girl my age. I was smitten with Fatooma and we played together until we turned ten. Then Fatooma was no longer allowed to come out to play, and my mother said to me, "You are too grown up to play like children now."

Mother was frugal and a good home manager, as many of the women of her generation were. They were skilled at stretching their resources, making sure we were never without. She always laid aside stores and some cash *li yawm al 'uzah* (for a day of need). She also liked the proverb that her homemaking skills personified, *al shatra tighzel bi rigl humar*, meaning, the clever woman can spin without a spindle and make yarn even with the leg of a donkey. I wondered, why donkey? Was it to say that the leg of so lowly an animal as the donkey could be put to good use if one was resourceful? I am reminded of my friend Wassef who, unlike most Egyptians, praised the much maligned and abused donkey. Why do we insult someone by calling him a donkey, shouting, *"ya humaar!"* (you ass!)? Wassef, who in the 1950s was arrested for supposedly communist activity, said to me one day: "You know, Ali, the donkey is an admirable beast who has all of the qualities of a true revolutionary. Look at how patient, steadfast, resilient, brave, and intelligent he is! He is the ideal revolutionary and yet he rarely mutinies."

At home, we were well fed and clothed. My father went to a local tailor for our clothing needs. His name was Usta Zaki or 'Am Zaki (uncle Zaki), as we called him mingling affection and respect for an elder. He made my father's clothes, but the rest of the family was clothed by the seamstress Sitti Fadila, who came to the house to sew for us. She stayed a week or ten days, slept, ate, and worked in our home until the boys and girls had been outfitted for the year. Some outfits, if they were still good, were handed down from child to child, or they were given away if they did not fit anyone. This was common practice in middle-class Egyptian families.

My mother had a Singer sewing machine that popped out of an oak table and had a foot with curlycues that I liked to play as a child. Sitti Fadila and my mother measured us, cut patterns, made dresses, shirts, nightgowns, and pajamas from all kinds of fabric; they cut, pinned, basted, laughed, drank tea, and sewed and sewed and sewed. I observed Sitti Fadila's feet, which were like a pair of fat wings going back and forth on the treadle. At dusk, my mother made her quit, and when she had completed the job, she was paid and we were outfitted for the year. Now my sister has that same Singer and it still works. Such times spent close to my mother and sisters are times in my life that I remember with great happiness.

My mother was taught how to read, write, and count, but otherwise did not have any formal education to speak of. She had common sense, was a natural with figures, and her eyes held so much intelligence that you knew she could have accomplished much in the world outside the home if she had been given the chance. She was kind and fair and made sure to teach her children right from wrong, leading mostly by example. My father, on the other hand, told us what to do and not to do.

My parents were related and grew up in the same building until my father built the apartment building to which they moved in the 1930s and where I was born. My father was older than my mother and had known her all her life. When I asked him if theirs had been an arranged marriage, he said yes, but that he had always loved her and had it in his mind to marry her as soon as she came of age. This desire fueled his ambition to better himself.

"When your mother turned sixteen, I went to my mother and asked her to speak for me. So she invited your grandmother and great aunts to tea then my father went to ask her father. We knew them, of course, because we were related, and so our fathers did not need to look into family reputations or any of the customary preliminaries. Then we were married."

I will describe my parents' appearance and my own. They were both tall and more fair skinned than dark. My mother had wavy, honey-colored hair and eyes. My father's were hazel, as are mine. I have inherited my great grandfather's darker complexion, however, and as I spend a lot of time in the sun on location, I am quite tan, *asmar*. Like my parents, I am tall, and my hair has a hint of the honey color in my mother's, though it is kinky whereas hers was smooth.

In Egypt certain traits are considered more desirable in a man than in a woman. You may notice that in ancient Egyptian paintings the man is often represented with a dark-reddish color whereas the woman is more a creamy yellow color. Another desirable attribute in our present-day culture is straight hair. Where this preference came from, I am not sure, because you see that the wigs worn by our ancestors are kinky or wavy, obviously a preference. Perhaps this disdain of dark skin and kinky hair came down to us in more recent history from the invading

Turks (and Europeans), who were fair skinned and often had light-colored eyes and silky hair, what Egyptians refer to with awe as *sha'r sayeh* (hair that is liquid). These racial preferences surely intruded on the Egyptian psyche, leaving an indelible mark. Often, to compliment a woman's beauty, people will say, "She looks Turkish." What nonsense!

My father dressed in the traditional manner of his day in wool kaftans topped by an overcoat, a crimson *tarboosh* (fez) tilted to one side on his head. He left the house each morning after prayers and after my mother sat with him as he drank a single cup of strong, black coffee, *fingaal ahwa saada*. He ate breakfast around 10 o'clock at the shop and ordered tea from the coffeehouse across the street. He ordered tea for his better clients as well, as was the custom, and always came home for lunch and a nap. He reopened the shop in the late afternoon and closed at 10 p.m. He performed his prayers wherever he was.

My mother dressed modestly but never wore the *hijab* (Islamic dress or veil). This style was not the customary dress of her day, as it has been since the 1970s. She did not believe that Islam required wearing it nor did she believe that a woman needed to hide her face. My father was of the same mind. When she went out, she wore a waisted, ankle-length dress and a *tarha* (long, gauzy, black scarf) draped over a matching *mandeel* (head wrap). This underscarf was a square of crepe de chine tied snugly around her head to hold her hair in. At home, she wore long, loose, print dresses and a white *mandeel*, decorated with a crocheted border. She was beautiful, graceful, and natural in her beauty and grace.

My mother and father's faith in God was expressed in their everyday lives, and their days were punctuated with prayer. They also practiced the personal responsibilities incumbent on every Muslim. I believe this lent serenity to their demeanor. In my mother's case, this calm also added to her feminine beauty. She and my father never raised their voices, and when they stood side by side they made a striking couple. My parents held steadfastly to all the teachings of Islam: prayer, fasting, alms-giving. Both taught us that if you had extra, it was not only your duty but also necessary for your salvation to practice *zakat*, a form of charitable giving to ease the burdens of other Muslims. My father used to say: "*Zakat* was taught and practiced by the Prophet Muhammad himself, *sala 'alayhu was sallam* (may peace be upon him). It is our duty to follow his example." Mother never turned away anyone who came to her door hungry or asking for alms. The resources she put aside, *li yoom al 'uzah*, went in part to alms.

By living the five pillars of Islam, our parents taught their children the *shahadah*, declaring that there is no God but God and that the Prophet Muhammad is his messenger. They taught us *salat*, prayer five times daily, and *zakat*, giving a portion of one's income to the poor. During the holy month of Ramadan we joined our parents in fasting, *sawm*, a practice that taught us self-control. Finally, we were taught about the *hajj*, the pilgrimage to the holy city of Mecca. It is every Muslim's heart's desire to make this pilgrimage at least once in a lifetime and it is also an obligation. Before I married, I did.

Until the age of ten, I attended a Catholic school and some of my teachers were Italian nuns. I don't know how my parents came up with this choice of school, but the experience familiarized me with different kinds of people and served me well when I worked as an Egyptian production manager on foreign films shot in Egypt. At this school we wore black uniforms and Sunday, not Friday, was the weekend. My sister's son attended that school too, and one day in 1952 we came home to find his father waiting for us at the front gate of the apartment building. He had a folded sheet of paper in his hand that he gave us, saying, "Run to the shop with this and don't give it to anyone but your father, Ali." My cousin did, and my father read the message out loud to us. King Farouk of Egypt had been deposed in a bloodless coup and we were to become a republic. My father was excited and, young as I was when this happened, I felt a sense of national pride and a desire to be part of this change. I understood even then that a revolution meant more equality: no king and subjects, no master and servant. I wanted to see a better Egypt for all.

Egypt began its budding efforts as a republic led first by Muhammad Naguib and then by Gamal Abdel Nasser, who in 1956 nationalized the Suez Canal, gaining for Egypt the huge revenues collected by ships passing through the canal. It was a huge step for Egypt, in which the United States sided with us as we ousted the occupying French and British.

Soon after, Israel made incursions into the Sinai, and in 1967, after a six-day war with Egypt, they defeated us. *Al naqsa* (the setback or calamity), as we called this dark day, profoundly marked my generation. We had sung songs like *Batal al thawra* (Hero of the revolution), a patriotic song praising Gamal Abdel Nasser as our leader: "Gamal, Gamal, hero of the revolution, defender of the rights of every man, Gamal, Gamal, treasure of our nation, jewel of our hearts lead us on to victory . . ." Alas, it was defeat, not victory, that awaited us when, in a single day, Israel destroyed our entire air force. After dreaming that marble statues would grace our canals, electricity would illuminate every village, concert halls would welcome musicians in every town, every citizen would own a car, abundance and equality would be ours, we were shattered. Many never recovered from the shock and the depression caused by this crushing defeat. I was depressed but resolved to carry on. I went to film school, and when I was thirty-five, I met my wife. This latter event was serendipity. I will tell you how it happened.

She and I met through friends a few months before I was rushed to the hospital for an appendectomy. When she heard of my surgery, she came to visit me and brought flowers. I was touched by her gesture, and when I was released I went to see her. After a time, I asked her to marry me and she accepted. So I went to see her parents. My parents had no objections. I remember saying to them, "I am thirty-five. Perhaps God brought us together for a reason, and it is to start a family." My parents agreed. She was from a good family, she was attractive and could converse pleasantly. She seemed to get along with my parents and I liked her family well enough. Because of her visit to the hospital, I thought her sensitive too. She was certainly feminine in appearance and in her demeanor, her comportment a little formal, which I liked. "This must be God's will," I thought, and so we were married.

Two years after our wedding and over my vigorous objections, she decided to become a *muhagaba*, to wear the *hijab*. She purchased long skirts and long-sleeved blouses and long kaftans as well as several sets of headscarves, veils, and gloves. She has dressed in this way ever since and I could not persuade her that if I had wanted to marry a *muhagaba* I would have chosen a *muhagaba*. This change meant that she did not want to see anyone but family and old friends. She refused to go with me on occasions when I socialized with foreign visitors or with people from the film industry. I couldn't help thinking, "Who wants to go home to a wife who has to pull on her gloves to shake hands!" We have stayed married for the sake of the children and lead different lives, going out together only for family gatherings.

As my wife and I spend less and less time together, I spend more and more time working and with friends. I teach a film class, I have built up a good reputation as a production manager, and I am well respected among film directors. I travel a good deal for my work. I pray and fast as did my parents and I believe my word to be my bond. I have accepted my wife as she is and she has realized that she cannot change me. This is how we keep the peace between us.

In conclusion, I can tell you that the worse time in my life was Egypt's defeat. The happiest time was growing up and also now when I am working. I thank God, and this is my story.

Mohammad Maghrabi

Fishing is my life. I have been fishing since I was a boy, and my boat is a fishing boat, just a rowboat. The number painted on the side shows that it has passed inspection and is licensed. It has no name. We leave the naming of boats to the ones who own *fellucas*. My boat is about 8 meters long. It was built in the town of Mansura, where a lot of boatbuilding takes place. It is made from the wood of the *kafur*, the eucalyptus, and it was my father who had it built for me.

My wife, Naima, lives with me on the boat. Our daughter Reda lived with us until she grew up and got married. When Naima was ready to give birth to Reda, I took her back to our village. One has to care for one's wife when putting a new soul into the world. A boat is no place for giving birth if you have a place to go and a family in a village to tend to a new mother and babe.

You asked me to tell you about fishing and so I will tell you about fishing. We fish using lines and hooks. Also we use a gill net that we call the *shannaka*, strangler. This net is about 300 meters long and 3 meters wide and is attached along one single rope studded with corks on one side and led pellets on the other. When we cast it, it forms a wall across the river because the one side is weighted, which causes it to sink to the bottom. It is like a wall that the fish swim into. It catches them by the gills and they cannot free themselves. They are strangled, which is why this net is called *shannaka*. I use two hands to cast this net. With the right hand, I cast the line with corks and with the left hand the line weighted with lead. Meanwhile, Naima rows downstream and goes back and forth across the river so that the net fans out in the water. We catch mostly small or medium-sized fish with the *shannaka* and lift them out of the net one by one. When we are not using the *shannaka*, we fan it out and fold it on the stern of the boat.

Al muhayyara, the befuddler, is a small, triple-layered net. The top and bottom layers have large openings, whereas the middle net is fine. It confuses the fish when they swim into the top nets and they get caught in the finer net and cannot swim back out. When we bring in this net, we open up the layers and slide out the fish.

Al na'ariyya, the trapper, is like the *muhayyara* but bigger. It is 50 meters long and 1 meter wide. It also hangs from a cork-studded rope, the corks spaced about half a meter apart. The lead pellets used to sink the net into the water are a man's handbreadth apart. We also use gourds on either side of the net to keep it afloat and identify ours from other fishermen's nets. The net sinks down and forms a vertical wall. Naima and I stand on the side of the boat and begin to drum on the side with sticks. The noise scares the fish away from the noise and into the layers of net where they get trapped, catfish often.

Al raddaakha, the breather, is another three-layered net we use. We stake this net to the riverbank and stretch it out as we move the boat out to let it fan out. The part of the net closest to shore sinks down. There are no corks to float it. The rest of the net fans out and forms pockets. When the water moves, the pockets move with it, and when fish swim into these pockets, they cannot get back out. It is called *raddaakha* because when the water moves it the pockets seem to breathe and puff up, then lie back down again, then breathe and puff up, and lie back down, and so on. The net moves with the movement of the water and traps the fish coming across it.

The *gubya* is a trap that has been outlawed because it threat-ened spawning fish. It is about half a meter long. It has a fine net in the shape of a funnel, which is secured with wires and dropped down into the river's bottom. A gourd marks the place where it has been placed, and once fish swim in there to spawn, they cannot go back out through the trap doors. Some fishermen still use it, but if they are caught, they are fined and the trap is confiscated.

And then there is the *madda*. We use this one most often and can leave it out overnight. It is about 100 meters long with fifty or so small lines hanging from it, with hooks on the small lines, about 2 meters apart. We call the main line the *'asab* (nerve) or the *dahr* (spine). We bait the hooks with *shirr al bulti*, which are the eggs of the white Nile fish. This bait we keep in a can with holes punched in its bottom and suspend the can halfway in the water to keep the bait from drying. I bait the hooks and Naima rows. While she rows, I drop each line into the water, gradually "feeding" the entire line to the river. Or else I row and Naima feeds. When I am ready to bring up the lines, I trawl for them with the *hilb* (anchor) and pull them in gradually while Naima unhooks the fish. In winter, a lot of the catch is eel.

Fishing with *sennaaret al khaytan* (threads) you need no bait. This is a line with smaller lines dangling from it, with hooks on the end of these smaller "threads." With this one we catch fish *bil lutsh*, which literally means by slapping them. The main line is stretched across the river with corks attached to every seventh thread. One end of the main line is secured to a big stone, then smaller stones, gradually getting smaller and smaller, are tied all along the line, which then floats at an angle; it sinks deepest into the water where the stones are bigger and floats higher in the water as the stones get smaller. The line dances in the water, and as it dances the threads ensnare the fish by slapping them and they get stuck on the hooks. You need three people to work this line, which is the sister line to *al madda*. The hooks on this line are made in Japan instead of at Dalganun, or Kafr al Zayyat, in the Delta region where a lot of fishing gear is made. Two people drop this line and one person pulls it up and wraps it around a pole attached to the boat with the fish still on the hooks. They will be removed once the entire line is in and coiled around the pole on the boat. The line must not get tangled and must be very carefully coiled around the pole, and the fish can then be unhooked; mullet, perch, tilapia.

There is also the *sarima*. It is a nylon line and the hooks are imported. The *sarimaat*, or shorter lines, are attached to the mother line. They are 20 to 30 centimeters long, placed 1 meter apart. They are also weighted by stones every ten hooks. We bait the hooks with half a kilo of worms each time it is cast. If the fish are biting, particularly in summer, fishermen might cast as many as three times, collecting the lines at sunset, or leaving them overnight, communicating their drop off points to one another to avoid tangled lines. You can catch a lot of fish in this way.

Now I have told you about fishing on the Nile and I can say *Toota toota firghit al haddootah* (a rhyme customarily used to end a folktale or a children's story) and begin another story, the story of my life, which you have asked me to tell you.

First I will tell you that Naima and I are from the same village. Our parents were peasants. This is true of most of the people fishing on the Nile. My older brother was the first to go out fishing and it was he who taught me how to fish. I would have gone back to the village to farm but my older brother died right after my father died and my middle brother took over the farm and ruined us. I had to make a living and so I continued on the river in Cairo, fishing.

I had a happy childhood and loving parents before my parents and my oldest brother died. I was sad then, especially after losing my mother. But Naima is now the light of my life and I accept God's will and thank God for his mercy. I was about thirteen years old when my father died. I did not feel the loss of him so much because my mother was alive. You see, her nearness and dearness were my consolation. As long as she was alive that was enough for me. When my father died, I was already fishing on the Nile with my oldest brother, Ali. When I went home, my mother opened her arms to me and I fell against her chest and hugged and hugged and kissed her. She brought the best of what she had in the house to feed me. It was her joy to have me near her and I could see the mother love on her face. Her love for me was such that it was as if I were her only child. Her tenderness and her kindness made me forget the loss of my father, who had been kind and gentle too. My mother drove any sadness out of my heart and far away from me.

When I was a small, I waited for my father to come home. I would run to greet him and dig around in his pockets for something good to eat, sweets or dates. He always had something for me in the pockets of his *galabeyya*. He laughed at my joy when I found them. So of course I was sad when he died. My brothers could not take his place. Then again, when you have one parent living you don't feel the loss of the other quite as sharply as you do when they are both gone. It was only when my mother died that I felt the real bite of grief. In fact, to this day, my heart aches and I never forget her. Of course, I had sisters, but they could not take her place nor could they equal a hair on my mother's head any more than 1 acre of land can equal 24 acres. I could ask my mother for anything because she was my mother. I could not ask my sisters and even less my sisters-in-law to as much as wash a cap or a handkerchief for me. They would resent it.

When I came home from the river and found my mother gone, I wept and could not eat. No one cares for you as do your parents, no one. But when I married Naima my heart began to heal, and when our daughter Reda was born and survived, she became as near and dear to me as my parents had been. I cherish her just as I was cherished by my parents. A cherished child grows up happy.

Growing up, we all slept in the same room. Mother spread straw mats on the swept dirt floor around the oven and this is where we slept. I sometimes slept on the flat top of the oven in winter because it was the warmest place to sleep. We slept near our parents until we grew up, and those of us who were old enough to marry, married and then slept with their wives or with their husbands.

In the village, our day began at dawn. Mother was first to rise. She milked the cow and the water buffalo and set aside the buffalo milk for us to drink after scooping the cream from the top. She then woke her eldest son's wife, whose job it was to knead flour and *samna* (clarified butter) to make biscuits for breakfast. We used only *samna* and knew nothing of oil. While my sister-in law made these preparations, we went on sleeping under the quilts. When she fired up the oven, we got up and folded the mats. The first to get up set out the breakfast, which was biscuits we dipped in cream. We were free to finish them or not to finish them. After breakfast, some of us who wanted to work in the fields, went. Others who had chores at home, stayed. We children were responsible for tending the animals and we tended them, leading them to the fields to eat *barseem* (alfalfa), which is why their milk was so rich and good. I was the youngest. I either played around the house or went to the fields with my older brothers and my father and tended the animals. At noon, mother brought lunch to us. She killed a chicken or made a meat stew, but always she fed us a hot meal. There was plenty of cheese that she made and stored in brine, which we ate with tomatoes, green onions, and *gargeer* (watercress and arugula), which grew by the irrigation ditches. We ate together and then made sweet tea, rested, and went back to work.

My brother and I were the first members of our family to become fishermen. Our grandparents had been farmers, as were our parents. They owned almost 1 *feddan* (acre) of land on which we grew four crops a year, one of them was *barseem* (alfalfa) the other three could be *kurumb* (cabbage), *lift* (turnips), and *bamia* (okra). Sometimes we grew red carrots.

We were four boys and three girls. It was easy to raise children then. Our parents brought us up in plenty, never neglected or hurt us. We did not know hardship as long as they were living. We had plenty to eat, clean clothes, and our food was always clean. When I was old enough to be parted from my mother, my father sent me to the *kuttab*, the Islamic school, where we were taught to memorize and recite verses from the Holy Qur'an. Sometimes our teachers visited us at home to hear us recite, knowing they would receive gifts of food when they came. There were two at the *kuttab*, one was mean one and one was kind. When the mean one came, I ran away and stayed in the fields. I disliked the *kuttab* anyway and did not want to be there. I preferred to be out in the fields. My father said to me, "Son, why don't you want to learn and be of some use to yourself?" I said, "I don't want to go to the *kuttab*, father, and I don't want to learn to recite and to spend my days reciting over dead men and their tombs."

My father did not insist that I return to the *kuttab*. He took me to work with him in the fields and taught me to walk behind the *gamoosa* (water buffalo) and the cow, to collect their dung and mix it with soil to spread as fertilizer on our fields, and to mix it with straw to fuel the oven. He taught me how to make these dung cakes and to dry them, even though this was usually women's work. Like all children, I thought I would live the rest of my life as a child and that my parents would always be near me.

My father wanted to give me a taste of hard work so I would ask to return to school, but I liked going to the fields and I liked working alongside him. I was well fed and happy and growing strong and I thought life would always be this way. Does anyone ever know what is waiting around the corner? I had not experienced hardship or unhappiness and knew nothing of the fire that burns a man's heart when he is poor or when death takes a loved one from him. I knew nothing of death until my parents died and I knew little of sadness until Naima and I lost two children. Thank God our one daughter Reda survived.

I was in the fields with my father when my oldest brother, Ali, went on the river. He went to help a neighbor who was a fisherman whose wife fished with him but was expecting her first child. The neighbor took his wife back to the village to give birth and took Ali out to help him. The neighbor expected to bring his wife back once she regained her strength and the baby could be safe out of doors. Ali took to the fishing life, however, and to life on the river, and did not want to come back to the village and farm, so my father had a boat built for him so he could go out on his own. I remember all of this. Father cut down a mulberry tree at the head of our field, and when the wood was ready, he hired a carpenter to build the boat. The cost was 4 Egyptian pounds at the time. When the boat was ready and licensed, my brother took me on as his helper and this is how I came to fish on the Nile.

When Ali made enough money to marry, he married a woman from town and took a factory job and left the fishing boat to me. When our father died, Ali went back to the village and took charge of the farm but soon died himself. That is when our troubles began. We had a cow, a buffalo, and our donkey had just given birth to a foal. After Ali died our middle brother took charge of the farm and the animals, but he was careless and lazy. He neglected the animals and they all died. On a very hot day he left the *gamoosa* with no water, and when he finally took her to drink she guzzled too much water too fast and died. We took her to the butcher, but he did not give us a good price for her, and what could we do? What happened to the *gamoosa*, happened to the cow. I was about eighteen then and was sending my earnings to my brother, but it was never enough. He was a waster and squandered everything and he let everything run down. Everything rotted and fell apart and we lost everything and we lost face in the village. Now when I went home it was not with my head held high as in my father's day. I was ashamed.

My brother married off the last of my sisters and thus had no more responsibilities, and he wanted me to get married as well and bring a wife home to help around the house. None of the brides he wanted for me was to my liking, and because of his recklessness—he spent like water—we found ourselves too impoverished for my prospects to be good. Things got from bad to worse and my brother eventually sold our land. Humiliation was wrapped around our name like a turban on a sheikh's head. What family would have me?

However, God works in his way and one day I saw the daughter of one of my uncles. It was Naima. Her face was like a full moon and she seemed not to worry about what people said. She took a liking to me, and I to her. We chose each other. I went to see one of her brothers to ask for her and he spoke to the eldest of the brothers and they agreed to marry Naima to me. The dowry was 30 Egyptian pounds.

I went back to the river, taking a young boy to help me fish, and at first Naima stayed in the village. I was catching plenty of fish and we had enough and were happy. I would leave the boy on the boat when I went to visit Naima in the village, and one day I was sleeping on the boat and saw in a dream that Naima had given birth to a son. I was very happy, but soon was sad because a few nights later I dreamed that the shirt I had left hanging on the hook at our house had disappeared and that people were washing a little body. I knew then that the baby had died. I got up and prayed, covered my boat, and got on a bus to go to the village.

When a neighbor saw me coming down the road, she clucked and clucked with her tongue. So it was true, my son had died. When I came in the door of our house I found Naima weeping. She wept when she saw me. I told her that God gives and takes away only what belongs to him and that we must accept our fate. She soon felt better and became pregnant again, this time with a baby girl who was stillborn. Then we had a third child who survived. Because Naima's mother had shouted "Reda" when the baby was born, we called her Reda, and she has been the apple of our eyes and the light of our lives. Reda means favor.

As time went on, it became hard to hire someone to help me on the boat. A lot of fishermen take their wives, but Naima was so pretty I worried about exposing her to that life and took the boat out of the water and went to work as a field hand on someone else's land. It was humiliating. The wage was 15 piasters a day, and I was not my own master. I endured two years of this, Naima asking all the while, "*Maalak*" (What is the matter)? I was downcast, but said to her, "It is God's will." What else could I say? Finally, when Reda was two, Naima pressed me to ready the boat and go back to the river, saying, "I will go with you." And so it was that we left for Cairo, taking Reda with us. We have lived on the river ever since that time.

I prepared a tarp to cover us for protection when we slept and Naima brought with her a basil plant and grew it in a can on the boat. She taps the leaves between her hands, inhales the fragrance, and declares: "Our year will be green just like this basil and God willing we will prosper." She always keeps basil growing on the boat. God has been kind to us and the fish have been plentiful. Naima took well to the fishing life and we raised Reda on the boat and we were happy. Other than the one time Reda fell over the side of the boat and I went in after her and fished her out, she grew up safe on the boat, but we attached a rope to her waist after the accident, just to be sure.

In Cairo, I did the shopping, going ashore for bread, rice, oil, vegetables, and once in a while meat. Of course I bought gas for the lamp and the Primus, and tea and sugar, which we must have to sustain us as we work. I also went to sell our fish. We fished and kept to ourselves as much as possible, avoiding anything more than the customary greetings and exchanges with other fishing families. When Naima was alone on the boat, she kept to herself to avoid trouble. We are vigilant in order to shield ourselves from gusts of unwanted attention and gossip: "*Al baab illi ye geeb il reeh, siddo wastareeh*" (the door from whence comes a draft, close it and insure your peace of mind).

When Reda grew up she married a soldier from our village. He took her back to the village to live with his family and was not kind. They deprived her of food, beat her, made her work like a servant to them, and did not treat her as they should have. Her husband sided with his mother and finally Reda complained and wanted to come back to us. She asked us to find a way to make her husband divorce her and we spoke to him, but he would not let her go.

Naima wept for Reda and decided to do something about her daughter's unhappiness. She went to a wise woman, one who knows, and paid her to help. She cast a spell on the boy and his family and we waited to see what would happen. They started to have problems and came running to us saying they would release Reda if we lifted whatever spell we had cast on them, and we agreed and went back to the village to get our daughter, her furniture, utensils, everything she had brought with her to her husband's house. Her in-laws objected and we called the police, and they put them in their place.

Someone had cast a spell on Reda and the spell was full of mischief and caused our daughter to become very sick. She shook and burned with fever, and soon after she and her mother went to a wise woman, who said, "The trouble between you and your husband dates back to the seventh day of your marriage. You have seen nothing but black days since that day and happiness has been a stranger to you." Reda asked, "Who was it who did this to me, Auntie?" The wise woman said, "It is one of your own blood. She paid a Sufi 15 pounds to make your husband hate you and she is the one who brought you soap and sweets at your wedding." Reda knew then that it was Naima's oldest sister. The wise woman said, "This relative filled a bundle with evil intent, which caused you to appear in the form of a monkey to your husband, and seeing you this way repulsed him. He couldn't stand to look at you, and his family was the same. She caused them to hate you."

Spells are powerful and are cast by those who know. The "ones who know" can be men or women, but there are more women than men involved, more women in the know, who work magic. I can tell you that if a wise woman wants to cast a good spell, she will depict someone as an angel or a queen, not a monkey. She will make a drawing on a paper or imagine it in her mind and she will conjure up protective walls around this person or build a beautiful room around her so that she can be safe and happy. She will write verses from the Qur'an, put them inside an amulet, or put them near to the person. But if she is casting a bad spell, she will depict her as a monkey or a *gamoosa* and leave her out in the open, exposed to the elements.

In the case of Reda, the wise woman said to her, "The one who did this to you did it to prevent you from taking root in any man's heart or home. She is jealous of you and of your mother. But beware, she won't show it. Be careful. She will pretend to pat you on the arm and to love you. Don't believe her. When you find the bundle, remove it, take it and put it in a bucket of water and set it out under the stars to 'star' it. It is the only way you will reverse the spell and its ill effects." As it turned out, a peasant was digging under a tree and found a bundle with some hair, nail parings, a string measuring Reda's height, and a paper with Reda's and Naima's names and the picture of a monkey all rolled up in a rag. The paper also had another name on it, "son of Hamida"—Hamida being Naima's sister—and her ill wishes written below her son's name: "May they never have peace in their hearts. May he always see her as a monkey. May happiness never enter their door." We were in the village and he came running to us with the bundle that he had taken to the village letter writer to read. That is how he knew it was meant for us. That very night, Naima took the bundle up to the roof of our house and placed it in a bucket of Nile water and left it there until dawn. She tossed out the water and refilled the bucket and did this three nights in a row. With each soaking, the spell grew weaker until on the fourth day Reda was delivered. Some people also burn a bundle into which a spell has been cast in order to harm someone, then mix the ashes with incense and ground coriander, then toss the mix into the air near an intended victim, who is then filled with hate and disquiet. Such victims hardly know if they are coming or going and blackness settles over them like a heavy cloud. A spell can also be cast into a glass of *karkade* (hibiscus drink) or tea. When drunk, it makes the intestines boil with the evil intent mixed in with the drink. Such a person can experience a violent dislike for the one named in the spell. Evil intentions can also be written on lemon leaves that are then burned. The person against whom the spell is directed suddenly burns inwardly.

You ask me how Reda's aunt got all of what she needed to put in that hate-filled bundle? Reda remembers. Hamida gave her a pair of scissors, patted and loved and kissed her, and said something like, "Here, cut your nails, Reda, my beauty. Be careful not to scatter the parings. Here, here, *ya ruhi* (my soul, dear heart), give them to me, I'll get rid of them safely for you," or something like this. In the countryside, one person is loving, ten are full of hatred, and a hundred are cunning!

When she was discovered, Naima's sister regretted her evil deed, but Naima remained cautious. And even though Reda shed the spell, the damage was done and between her and her husband there was no love or understanding. We pleaded with him to release her and he finally divorced her, but not until Naima had first put a spell on him that caused him to feel aches and pains, and of course when a child suffers the mother of the child suffers too. Naima's sister guessed the direction from which this ill wind was buffeting her son's body and came running to Naima to beg forgiveness. Naima agreed to help if her boy agreed to set free our daughter, and he did. And this is just how it happened.

Two years later Reda married a good man and she now lives in Cairo and our hearts no longer burn with worry for her. Naima and I continue to fish on the Nile and to go to the village from time to time, and sometimes Reda comes with us. We still have a house in the village and we still have understanding in our hearts and we get along and thank God Almighty for his mercy.

Afterword

Those who do not know history are condemned to repeat it." Those were the sage words of the philosopher George Santayana, then living in Spain in 1863. He is, of course, reflecting on some of the lessons that humanity has and, more often than not, has not learned from the tragedies and disasters of the past. In the context of today's Middle East, and specifically Egypt, the sentiment seems unfortunately apposite. To it I would append another observation, one that may have already been uttered by someone else unknown to me: Before you decide to be rid of a dictator and the system that he represents and controls, make sure that you have both a clear idea as to what or who will take his place and a method of carrying that out.

In the heady days that came after the events of January 2011, the misnamed "Arab Spring," initially in Tunis but then elsewhere throughout the Arabic-speaking world, the future seemed to augur well for those Egyptians of all ages who gathered in Tahrir Square in central Cairo (where the compiler of this telling series of life stories has lived). However, subsequent events—the apparently popular election of a new president from the Muslim Brotherhood, the intervention of the Egyptian Army, the removal and trial of that president, the subsequent rise to power and the presidency of an army commander, and the brutal suppression of all forms of opposition—have all suggested that the Egyptian people, who are well aware of their centuries-old history and have lived through prolonged eras of tyranny within that lengthy time frame, are now called on yet again to live a present and contemplate a future that both raise any number of questions. Is their current situation, they wonder, a case of "back to the 1950s and 60s"—an often tense and unhappy period when, incidentally, the writer of this Afterword was in Cairo? Can things be that bad again, they wonder, or is it, *yā Laṭīf* (O kind God), even worse now?

It is within the context of these questions (and, needless to say, many others) that this collection of essays—with its own interesting precedents and history—becomes especially valuable. Nayra Atiya herself asks the all-important questions in her Preface: Can the personal histories of these five Egyptian men shed some light on the twenty-first century? On how current events unfolded—the 2011 and 2013 uprisings, for example?

The very title of this collection, *Shahaama*, with its accounts of five Egyptian lives, reflects a value that has long been regarded as an intrinsic part of an Egyptian's self-identity: a sense of honor, one based on a set of values that, as this book clearly shows, may no longer prevail in many decision-making processes to the extent that it once did—an impression only enhanced by the lives and memories of these five Egyptians. One important facet of this volume, like its predecessor, *Khul-Khaal: Five Egyptian Women Tell Their Stories* (1982), is that Nayra Atiya can look at the lives of Egyptians, today and yesterday, through the double lens of a native Egyptian who has not only lived an Egyptian life (you cannot get much closer than a houseboat on the Nile and an apartment close to the center) but has also resided outside the city in the village of Shabramant, near the Giza pyramids, on the Elephantine Island in Aswan, in Alexandria, as well as in Europe and the United States. The valuable quality that such a profile provides is that of perspective, and it is much in evidence in this book, not only in her own Introduction but also in the way the stories of the men involved are sequenced and structured.

The choice of these particular Egyptian men also offers another sense of perspective; most important, perhaps, of different religious communities: three Muslims, one Jew, and one Copt, the oldest established Christian congregation in the world (the word "Copt," like "Egypt," being connected with the ancient Egyptian God, Ptah) and the faith community of Atiya herself. The connections of these five men with Egypt and abroad, their professions, their levels of education, their places of birth and residence, and their attitudes toward the past are all interestingly varied and well captured (and interestingly, except for Mohammad Maghrabi, the fisherman, their names are disguised in order to avoid any political or social problems that might arise as a result of their frank expression of opinions). It is equally clear that Nayra Atiya is willing to confront controversy, in that her decision to include among the five an Egyptian-born Jew and Zionist who was to be deported from Egypt (although his parents remained in Alexandria) has already been questioned. In her response she notes that "he represents one of the many faces of Egypt, providing a noteworthy vignette of a moment in its history and the history of one of its once-vital communities"—shades, one might suggest, of the scenario portrayed in Lawrence Durrell's famous novel (the first of his Alexandria quartet), *Justine* (1957).

The chapters devoted to these five Egyptian men provide the reader with an authentic and vivid picture of a Middle Eastern country—Egypt—that, during the course of those same lives, has borne witness, often painful witness, to the impact of colonialism, globalization, conflict (at least three wars with the Israeli state), industrialization, capitalism, terrorism, and political and social change; to uncontrollable increases in population, ever-expanding cities, and grotesque differences in lifestyle; to deposed kings and presidents who die of natural causes, are assassinated, and, most recently, are ousted and tried; but also to that enduring Egyptian spirit (accompanied by a renowned tradition of humor) that is so well represented by the concept of *shahaama*. All the factors that lend themselves to any knowledgeable discussion of the present and future of Egypt are present, in one way or another, on these pages, and that makes for a truly precious contribution to debates on the still-unclear prospects for Egypt in the first instance but thereafter for the Middle East as a whole.

August 2015   Roger Allen

NAYRA ATIYA is an American oral historian, writer, and translator born in Egypt. She lives on the Canaveral Coast of Florida. Her first book, *Khul-Khaal: Five Egyptian Women Tell Their Stories*, won a UNICEF prize in 1990 and has been widely translated. Her sixth book, *France Davis: An American Story Told*, won the 2006 Utah Book Award in nonfiction. This is her seventh book.